AF512772

Philosophical Foundations of Education

Philosophical Foundations of Education

JAGDISH CHAND
Former Deputy Director of Education and
Executive Director of the Delhi Bureau of Textbooks,
Delhi Administration

ANSHAH

Anshah Publishing House

All rights reserved. No part of this work may be reproduced, stored in a retrieval system or transmitted in any form or by any means, electronic, mechanical, photocopying, recording or otherwise without the prior written permission of the copyright owner and publishers.

Rs. 750; US$ 25

ISBN: 978-81-8364-060-2

2014 Impression
(2010)

Philosophical Foundations of Education

© Reserved

Published by:

ANSHAH PUBLISHING HOUSE
LG 18-19, Pankaj Central Market,
Patparganj, Delhi 110092, Ph.: 22235152, 22236152
Email: info@shiprapublication.com
Website: www.shiprapublication.com

Preface

The book 'Psychological Philosophical and Sociological Foundations of Education', published in 2009 covers the emerging concerns in education presented by the changing philosophical, psychological and sociological perspectives.

As per the demand in the market and requirement of curriculum in various universities, the book covering philosophical foundations of education is brought out independently. It is hoped that this volume will be welcomed by the readers and its advantage is also taken by the pre-service and in-service teachers.

Wide range of primary and secondary sources has been consulted and used for enriching the book, author is grateful to all the authors and their publishers.

Jagdish Chand

Contents

1

Basic Ideas in Education

SIGNIFICANCE OF EDUCATION

According to thinkers in ancient India, *Vidya* or knowledge or learning or education is the 'third eye' of man, which gives him an insight into all affairs and teaches him how to act; it leads us to our salvation; in the mundane sphere it leads us to all-round progress and prosperity. The illumination given to us by *Vidya* shatters illusion, removes difficulties and enables us to realise the true value of life. A person who does not possess the light of education, may be really described as blind. The correct insight, which men and women get from *Vidya*, naturally increases their power and efficiency. The uses of *Vidya* are too diverse to be enumerated exhaustively; it nourishes us like the mother; directs us to the proper path like the father; and gives us delight and comfort like the wife. It increases our fame; and makes us pure and more cultural. When we are in the solitude of a journey, or in a foreign country, it serves us as a valued companion.

According to a Sanskrit verse, education sharpens the intelligence makes our speech truthful, increases our fame, keeps us away from sin, delights us and spreads our name in all directions. It is like *Kalpavriksha*—a veritable desire-yielding tree.

The following verse is a common saying in India.

Swadesh pujayate raja
Vidyavan sarvatra pujyata

(A king is respected in his own kingdom while a learned man is worshipped everywhere).

The *Hindu law* givers observe that the very sight of a learned man is sacred.

The *Rig Veda,* the most ancient book in the world states, "Education is the source of all illumination".

The *Upanishadas* tell us, "Through education one enjoys the fruit of immortality".

Aristotle (384-322 BC), a famous Greek philosopher has said, "Educated men are as much superior to the uneducated as the living to the dead".

Diogenes (4th Century BC), a great cynic Greek philosopher writes, "Education is a controlling grace to the young, consolation to the old, wealth to the poor and ornament to the rich".

Epicetus (1st, 2nd Century A.D.), states "Only the educated are free".

Joseph Addison (1672-1719), an English essayist and poet believes, "What sculpture is to a block of marble, education is to human soul".

The Education Commission 1964-66, the first Commission in independent India which examined all the facets of education at all levels very aptly began its report with these words, "The destiny of India is now being shaped in her classrooms. This we believe, is no more rhetoric. In a world based on science and technology, it is education that determines the level of prosperity, welfare, and security of the people. On the quality and number of persons coming out of our schools and colleges will depend our success in the great enterprise of national reconstruction whose principle objective is to raise the standard of living of our people".

The National Policy on Education 1986 and as slightly modified in 1992 has also observed, "The country has reached a stage in its economic and technical development when a major effort must be made to derive the maximum benefit from the assets already created and to ensure that the fruits of change reach all sections. Education is the highway to that goal". Again it states, "In our national perception education is essentially for all. This is fundamental to our all-round development, material and spiritual. In sum, education is a unique investment in the present and the future".

DIVERGENT VIEWS ON THE MEANING OF EDUCATION

The word education has a very wide connotation. It is like a diamond which appears to be of a different colour when seen from a different angle. Like the concept of the proverbial elephant as described by blind men, an artist, a biologist, an economist, an educator, a philosopher, a political leader, a psychologist, and a sociologist etc. seems to have his own concept and meaning of education which are influenced by his own outlook of life.

ETYMOLOGICAL MEANING OF EDUCATION

Etymologically, the word 'education' is derived from the following Latin words which are briefly explained here:

(i) *Educare*. This means 'to raise', 'to nourish', 'to bring up'.
(ii) *Educere*. This implies 'to draw out', 'to lead out'.
(iii) *Educatum*. This denotes 'to train'.
(iv) *Educo*. 'e' meaning 'out of', and 'duco' meaning 'to lead', 'to lead out'.

Thus education means:

(i) to bring up
(ii) to draw out
(iii) to lead out
(iv) to nourish
(v) to raise
(vi) to train

A synthesis of the meaning of these terms implies that

education is drawing out and leading out something from within the individual by bringing up, nourishing, raising and training him.

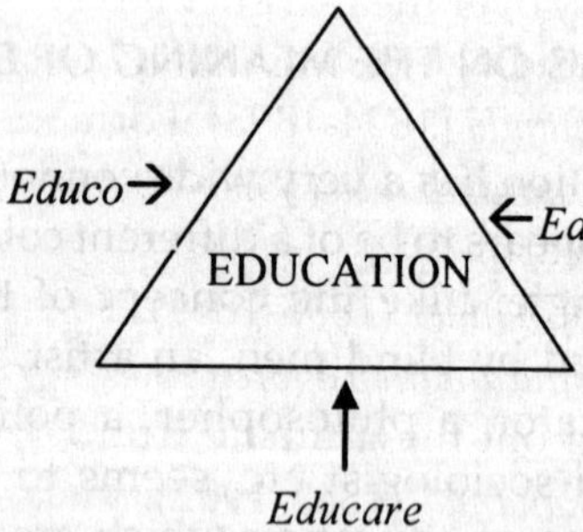

Fig. 1.1: Showing the Origin of the term Education (Derivation or Etymology of Education)

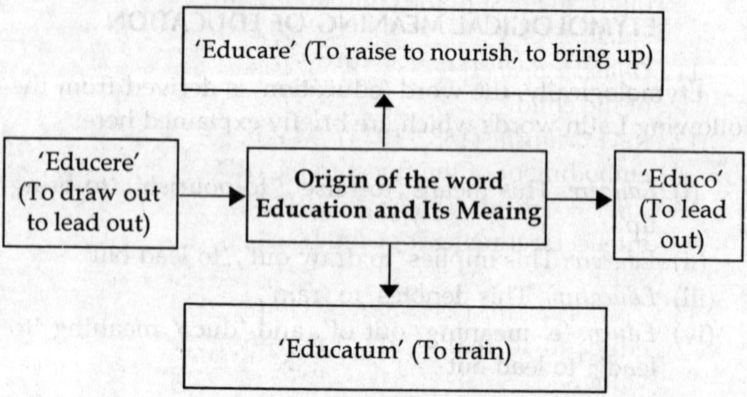

Fig. 1.2: Showing the Origin of the Word Education and its Meaning

GREAT INDIAN AND WESTERN THINKERS ON THE MEANING OF EDUCATION

A. Views of Great Indian Thinkers on Education

1. *Yajnavalkya* (About 1600 B.C.). Bringing together of the individual and the Supreme.
2. *Chanakya/Kautilya/Vishnu Gupta* (4th Century B.C.). Training for the love of the country.

3. (*Swami*) *Sankaracharya* (788-820 A.D.). Realisation of the self and attainment of *Moksha* (Liberation).
4. (*Guru*) *Nanak Dev* (1469-1539). Enabling an individual to win victory over the five enemies – lust, anger, greed, infatuation and ego (*Kam, Krodh, Lobh, Moh, Ahankar*).
5. *Swami Dayananda* (1824-1893). Formation of character.
6. *Ramakrishna Paramhansa* (1836-1886). Purification of the mind and heart.
7. *Sen., Keshub Chander* (1838-1884). To develop morality.
8. *Gurudev Rabindranath Tagore* (1861-1941). Enabling the mind to find out the ultimate truth.
9. *Swami Vivekananda* (1863-1902). Manifestation of the perfection already in man.
10. (*Mahatma*) *M.K. Gandhi* (1869-1948). All-round drawing out of the best in the child and man—body, mind and spirit.
11. *Gijubhai Badheka* (1885-1939). Fashioning the emotion of the child.
12. *K.M. Munshi* (1887-1974). Making a young man an embodiment of the finest in his culture.
13. *Radhakrishnan Sarvapalli* (1888-1975). Training the intellect, refinement of the heart and discipline of the spirit.
14. *Zakir Hussain* (1897-1969). Helping the mind of the educand to realise absolute moral and intellectual value.
15. *J. Krishnamurti* (1895-1986). Understanding of oneself for it is within each one of us that the whole of existence is gathered.

B. Views of Great Western Thinkers in Education

1. *Socrates* (469-399 B.C.). Dispelling error and discovering truth.
2. *Plato* (427-347 B.C.). Developing the body and the soul of all the perfections which they are capable of.
3. *Quintilian* (38-86 A.D.). Character as the end of education.

4. *Erasmus, Desiderius* (1466-1536). Developing real wisdom.
5. *Montaigue, Michel Eyqueen De* (1533-1592). Cultivating manners, behaviour and judgement than bare and mere liberal learning.
6. *Comenius, John Amos* (1592-1670). Development of the whole man.
7. *Milton, John* (1608-1674). Fitting a man to perform justly, skilfully and magnanimously all the official, both private and public of peace and war.
8. *Locke, John* (1632-1704). Attainment of a sound mind in a sound body.
9. *Kant, Immanuel* (1724-1804). Man-making education.
10. *Rousseau, Jean Jacques* (1712-1878). Development from within.
11. *Pestalozzi, Johann Heinrich* (1746-1827). Natural, harmonious and progressive development of innate powers.
12. *Schiller, Fredrich* (1759-1805). Process of emotional development.
13. *Herbart, Johann Friedrich* (1776-1841). Developing morality.
14. *Froebel, Friedrich* (1782-1852). Leading and guiding for peace and unity with God.
15. *Mann, Horace* (1796-1859). Educating children in the great eternal principle of justice and might which underline the entire length of human existence.
16. *Emerson, Ralph Waldo* (1803-1883). Controlling the mind.
17. *Huxley, Thomas Henry* (1825-1895). Fashioning the will of the individual to enable him to move in harmony with nature.
18. *Parker, Francis Wayland* (1837-1902). Realisation of all the possibilities of human growth.
19. *Ruskin, John* (1819-1900). Developing physical health, manual and moral training.

20. *Spencer, Herbart* (1820-1903). Preparing for complete living.
21. *Tolstoy, Count Leo Nikolayevich* (1828-1910). Providing freedom in learning.
22. *Kilpatrick, William Heard* (1871-1925). Enabling the child full participation in the richest available group life.
23. *Nunn, T. Percy* (1870-1944). Complete development of the individuality of the child so that he can make an original contribution to human life according to the best of his capacity.
24. *Whitehead, Alfred Worth* (1861-1947). Assimilation of general ideas which could be applied to life.
25. *Santayana* (1863-1952). Providing liberal education to a minority and teaching the three R's to the masses.
26. *Tolstoy, Count Leo Nikolayevich* (1828-1910). Providing freedom in learning.
27. *Dewey, John* (1859-1952). Increasing social efficiency.

ANALYSIS OF SOME DEFINITIONS OF EDUCATION

1. One of the oldest treatises on education entitled *The Great Learning*, written around 2,500 years ago and attributed to Confucious, a great Chinese scholar and thinker sets out the meaning, the aim and the process of education in these words, "The great learning consists in manifesting the clear character, loving the people and abiding in the highest grid. Those who wish to make their wills sincere would first extend their knowledge. The extension of knowledge consists in the investigation of things; when things are investigated, knowledge is extended; when knowledge is extended, the will becomes sincere, when the will is sincere, the mind is rectified, when the mind is rectified, the personal life is cultivated; when the personal life is cultivated, the family will be regulated; when the family is regulated, the state will be in order, and when the state is in order there will be peace in the universe". Although this definition does not make clear the meaning of terms like 'will', knowledge and cultivated etc. yet it seems to be an operational one.

2. According to Nunn, "Education is the complete development of the individuality so that he can make an original contribution to human life to his best capacity". The individual is a sum total of various constituents and all these must be developed. Every individual is a unique one and as such the task of education is to cater to the individual needs. The development should take place to the maximum possible extent. This definition takes note of the needs of other human beings also.

3. Thomson says, "By education I mean the influence of the environment upon the individual to produce a permanent change in his habits of behaviour, of thought and of his attitude. Environment has various aspects—physical, social and cultural. Education should facilitate the task of adaptation of the child to his environment". The definition highlights the need for providing a suitable environment.

4. According to Redden, "Education is the deliberate and systematic influence extended by the mature person upon the immature through instruction, discipline and harmonious development of the physical, intellectual, aesthetic, social and spiritual powers of the human being according to their essential hierarchy by and for the individual and social uses, and directed towards the union of the educand with the creator as the final end". The ultimate goal of life is the union of the individual with God. This union can take place only when the various capacities of the child are developed for the good of the individual as well as that of society.

This definition points out the three-fold function of the educator. One, for the development of powers of the individual. Two, for enabling the individual to become a useful member of the society. Three, for assisting the individual to be one with the Creator. In other words, education should liberate the individual. The objective of life as attainment of *'Moksha'* as advocated by ancient Indian seers is emphasised in this definition.

5. Aristotle's definition neglects the spirit and education is only in terms of creation of 'a sound mind in a sound body'.

6. Gandhiji observed, "By education I mean an all-round drawing out of the best in the child and man—body, mind and soul".

He has also stated, "True education is that which draws out and stimulates the spiritual, intellectual and physical faculties of the children".

The following points bring out the importance of the definition and meaning of education as given by Gandhiji.

Meaning of All-Round: Man is neither mere intellectual nor the gross animal body, nor the heart or soul alone. A proper and harmonious combination of all these is required for the making of the whole man.

Any programme of education that puts exclusive emphasis on one of these aspects of the human personality is against the basic principle of education.

Meaning of the term 'best in man': The best in man is related to three aspects: body, mind and spirit. No field should remain neglected. The best in man will include the harmonious development of all the three aspects or faculties of the child.

'Drawing out' and not 'Pouring in': has been stressed by Gandhiji. He wrote, "We have up to now concentrated on stuffing a child's mind with all kinds of information without even stimulating or developing them". He fully realised that nature has endowed children and youth with tremendous vitality. They have within them the springs of youth, joy and vigour. They have the God-given curiosity to wish to know things for themselves. The task of education is to use these powers. It would be wrong to suppress them. Their energy should be utilised and harnessed properly.

How can we draw out the best?: The best can be drawn out by touching the hearts of children. Gandhiji states, "If I was to be their real teacher and guardian, I must help them to solve the problems that faced them, and I must take along the right channel the surging aspirations of this youth".

Gandhiji further explained the concept of education in his book *Basic Education* as, "I hold that true education of the intellect can only come through a proper exercise and training of the bodily organs, e.g., hands, feet, eyes, ears, nose, etc. In other words an intelligent use of the organs in a child provides the best and quickest way of developing his intellect. But unless the development of the mind goes hand in hand with a corresponding awakening of the soul, the former alone would prove to be a poor lop-sided affair. By spiritual training I mean education of the heart. A proper and an all-round development of the mind, therefore, can take place only when it proceeds *pari passu* with education of the physical and spiritual faculties of the child. They constitute an indivisible whole".

For drawing out the best a suitable environment is needed in the family, the school, the community and the society.

FUNCTIONAL AND OPERATIONAL DEFINITION AND MEANING OF EDUCATION

By education we mean the natural, harmonious and progressive development of man's innate powers by drawing out the best in his body, mind and spirit so as to produce an individual who is culturally refined, emotionally stable, ethically sound, mentally alert, morally upright, physically strong, socially efficient, spiritually enlightened, vocationally self-sufficient and internationally liberal. This should be the end product of education. Any programme of education which puts exclusive emphasis on one of these aspects of the human personality will be considered as lop-sided and narrow. Broadly speaking, this functional and operational definition and meaning should guide us in planning and implementing our educational programmes (Fig. 1.3).

SARCASTIC AND NEGATIVE VIEW OF EDUCATION

"We thought the students wanted education, but all that they wanted was a degree".

"We thought they wanted a degree, but all that they wanted was a job".

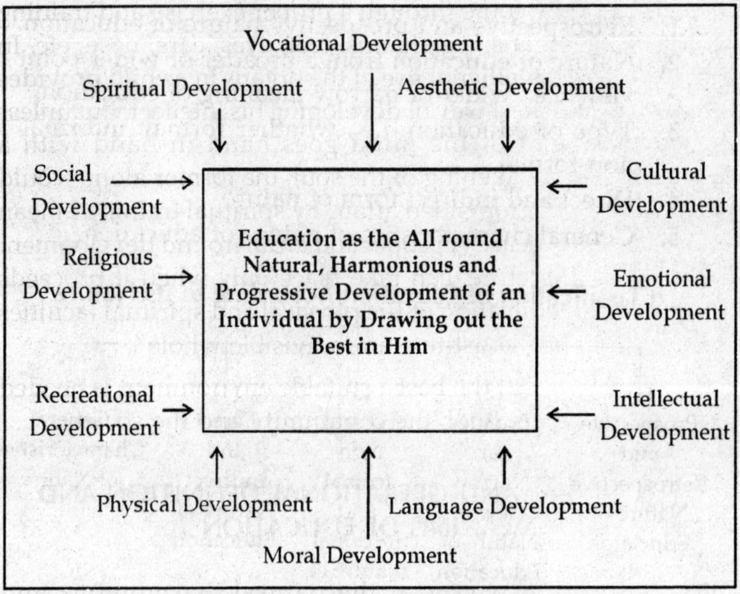

Fig. 1.3: Meaning of Education

"We thought they wanted a job, but all that they wanted was work".

"We thought they wanted work, but all that they wanted was money".

"We thought they wanted money, but all they wanted was money through fair or foul means". —*Anon*

Education makes machines which act like men and produces men who act like machines. —*Erich Fromn*

A man who has never gone to schools may steal from a freight car, but if he has university education, he may steal the whole rail road. —*F.D. Roosevelt*

NATURE OF EDUCATION

There are several ways of explaining the nature of education. In this regard following points deserve consideration:

1. Retrospective and prospective nature of education.
2. Nature of education from a broader or wider point of view, i.e., wider or narrow meaning of education.
3. Type of education, i.e., whether formal, informal or non-formal.
4. Direct and indirect form of nature.
5. General characteristics of nature of education.

Classification of Education According to its Nature

(1) Prospective and Retrospective Nature of Education

(2) Broader or Narrow view of Nature of Education

(3) Formal, Non-formal and Informal Nature of Education

(4) Direct and Indirect Nature of Education

(5) General Characteristics of Nature

RETROSPECTIVE AND PROSPECTIVE NATURE OF EDUCATION

Education is both retrospective and prospective. It is both conservative and progressive. Education transmits the culture of one generation to another. The rising generation has not only to be conveyed the activities and experiences of the past generation and asked to carry on those activities but it has to be asked to make necessary changes in these activities and experiences to meet the new situations with which it will meet. An integration of the old must take place with the new ones. It must be remembered that the communities live in the present on the past and for the future. This means that activities and experience in the present will guide the activities of the future. Thus education is continuous reorganisation and integration of activities and experiences. Education is a constructive agency for improving our society. Brown has stated, "Education brings changes in behaviour, and if its main functions are to remain mere transmission or enrichment of culture, it will fall short of its role in a dynamic society. Education must also provide situations at all age levels but within the maturity and ability of the individual to stimulate a creativeness of mind which can explore new horizons and bring the vision of the future into a living reality".

Education takes place when new ideas combine with the old. Something new is constructed by the synthesis of the two and this process goes on constantly and through life. Education is growth and growth never stops. We learn in terms of the old. An intelligent order, sequence and continuity is to be maintained as the new thing and best can be learnt in the context of the old one. Herbart's principle of 'appreciation' points out the same fact.

Child is active by nature. He plays and does so many things but these undifferentiated rich and practical experiences, do not lead to education unless they are guided and properly directed. So the experiences of the child should be given coherence, unity and organisation, and education is to be consciously and deliberately planned by providing rich and creative activities and experiences to children. The experiences of the child should be well-knit to give them meaning. Education is to bring about the growth of the educand through experience and activity. Every experience and activity leads to some sort of learning and enrichment of the mind of the learner. These in turn enter into combinations and thus increase the ability of the new learner to direct further noble activities and experiences.

CHIEF CHARACTERISTICS OF THE NATURE OF EDUCATION

Following are the chief characteristics of the nature of education:

1. *Education is Purposive, i.e.,* there is a definite purpose underlying all educational activities.
2. *Education is Deliberate, i.e.,* education involves care and guidance.

3. *Education is Planned, i.e.,* education is not haphazard. It is systematic.
4. *Education is Life-long, i.e.,* education starts from the time of conception and goes on till death—education from cradle to grave as is sometimes said.
5. *Education is Influence Exerted, i.e.,* the mature persons (parents, elders and teachers) influence the learners.
6. *Education is Balanced Development, i.e.,* education is concerned with the development of all faculties of the child.
7. *Education is Bi-polar, i.e.,* both the teacher and the pupil influence each other. Of course, the influence of the teacher is very prominent.
8. *Education is Tri-polar, i.e.,* education involves the teacher, the taught and the environment or the subject-matter.
9. *Education is Psychological as well as Social, i.e.,* the endowments or the capacities of the child—his needs, interests etc. must be interpreted in a social setting.
10. *Education is Growth, i.e.,* education modifies the behaviour of the child.

BROAD AND NARROW MEANING OF EDUCATION

Broad Meaning of Education

It is almost universally accepted that an individual educates himself so long as one breathes. Education of an individual begins from 'conception' and continues till 'cremation'. It goes on from 'womb' to 'tomb' or 'cradle' to 'grave'. Whatever broadens our horizon, deepens our insight, refines our emotions and stimulates our thought and feeling, educates us. It includes all influences, direct and indirect, formal and informal, deliberate or incidental, planned or unplanned. We learn whether we are conscious of this fact or not. Education includes all influences — cultural, domestic, economic, geographical, political, religious, social and spiritual.

According to William H. Kilpatrick, "From the broad point of view all life thoughtfully lived is education".

John Stuart Mill has stated the wider meaning of education in these words, "Not only does education include whatever we do for ourselves and whatever is done for us by others, for the express purpose of bringing us somewhat nearer to the perfection of our nature, it does more, in its largest acceptance, it comprehends even the indirect effects produced on character, and on human faculties, by things of which the direct purposes are quite different, by laws, by forms of government, by the industrial arts, by the modes of social life, nay even by physical facts not dependent on human will, by climate, soil and local position. Every environment, every surrounding, every activity helps to shape the human being. A human soul is in constant interaction with his environment. The interaction results in the modification of human behaviour or education".

R.C. Lodge explains the scope of education in his book *Philosophy of Education* which deserves careful consideration. "In the wider sense, all experience is said to be educative. The bite of a mosquito, the taste of watermelon, the experience of falling in love, of flying in an aeroplane, of being in a storm in a small boat—all such experiences have a direct educative effect on us. The child educates the parents, the pupil educates his teachers... Everything we say, think or do educates us no less than what is said or done to us by other beings, animate or inanimate. In the wider sense, life is education and education is life".

J.S. Mackenzie is of the view, "In the wider sense, it is a process that goes on throughout life and is promoted by almost every experience in life".

Dumvile writes, "Education in its widest sense includes all the influences which act upon an individual during his passage from cradle to grave".

The wider meaning of education includes all the meanings attached to formal, informal and non-formal education.

It is said that a pupil gets one-fourth of his education from his teacher, another fourth by his own intellectual efforts, another fourth from his fellow students and the rest in the course of time through life and experience.

The wider meaning of education includes the following:

1. The process of education is a lifelong process, from infancy to old age or from 'womb to grave'.
2. It includes experiences gained through the various formal and informal agencies of education. We learn from home, school, church, cinema, club, press, travel, friends, physical and social environments.
3. All experience is said to be educative.
4. We receive education many a time when we are not conscious of it.

Narrow Meaning of Education

To quote T. Raymont, "In the narrower sense in which the term is used in common speech and in legal enactments, education does not include self-culture and the general influence of one's surroundings, but only those special influences which are consciously and designedly brought to bear upon the younger by the adult population of the community, whether through the family, the church or the state".

J.S. Mill explains the narrow meaning of education as, "The culture which each generation purposefully gives to those who are to be its successors, in order to qualify them for at least keeping up, and if possible for raising the level of improvement which has been attained".

Prof. Drever explains the narrow meaning of education in these words, "Education is a process in which and by which knowledge, character and behaviour of the young are shaped and moulded".

G.H. Thompson's definition of education indicates the narrow view of education, "The influence of the environment on the individual with a view to producing a permanent change in the habits of behaviour, of thought and attitude".

Narrow meaning of education usually implies imparting

information or giving instruction or schooling or training, or making people literate, or teaching or preparing for a trade or vocation.

A.N. Whitehead is right when he says, "A merely well-informed person is the most useless bore on God's earth".

Narrow education includes special and specific influences. Education in a narrower sense means a conscious and deliberate process, well-planned to modify the behaviour of the educand in desirable and socially approved channels and to bring about in the educand specific knowledge and skills. This point is explained as under:

1. Narrow type of education is imparted in planned institutions like schools.
2. It is limited to the teaching of ready-made material.
3. Education is regarded as synonymous with instruction.
4. It is a deliberate, conscious and systematic influence exerted by the mature person, i.e., the teacher, on the immature person, i.e., the child.
5. This type of education is intentional rather than incidental.
6. Knowledge is considered as the accumulated experience of the human race. It is more or less fixed.

WHAT EDUCATION IS NOT AND WHAT EDUCATION IS?

1. *Literacy is Not Education*: Literacy is concerned with the traditional 3 R's, that is, reading, writing and arithmetic. It is related to acquiring knowledge of some subjects. Education, on the other hand, is related to 7 R's, that is, reading, writing, arithmetic, rights, responsibilities and their relationships and recreation.

Literacy is mainly concerned with theoretical knowledge which can be evaluated through different types of questions—essay type, short answer type and objective type. But education cannot be evaluated through these techniques. Education provides a way of life. It develops certain values. A person may possess high literacy and even high sounding degrees but he may be labelled uneducated if he lacks human qualities. Education is concerned with the development of character and personality.

2. *Education is not mere Schooling*: Education takes place within the four walls of the school and outside also. Education is not mere spending a few hours in the school and learning some subjects.

3. *Education is not information*: Information must lead to constructive thinking and wisdom.

4. *Education is not instruction*: Instruction is confined to classroom. Education is life-long and ends with death.

5. *Education is not indoctrination*: Indoctrination is confined to a particular belief but education is very broad and leads to broad mindedness.

6. *Education is not merely training of mind*: Education is concerned with the development of body, mind and soul.

FUNCTIONS OF EDUCATION

Education is expected to perform the following functions:

1. Individual development functions.
2. Social development functions.

Individual Development Functions of Education: These functions of education are:

(i) Maximum development of the innate or natural abilities and powers of individuals.
(ii) Development of character and personality of the individuals.
(iii) Preparing individuals for living present life amicably and happily.
(iv) Preparing individuals for taking up gainful employment/self-employment.
(v) Development of suitable leisure time pursuits.

(vi) Development of qualities of followership and leadership.
(vii) Development of emotions of individuals so that they are emotionally stable.

Social Development Functions of Education: These may be stated as:

(i) Development of skills of the individuals that help them to harness the natural resources of the country.
(ii) Development of community sense among the students.
(iii) Conservation of social heritage by providing suitable curriculum to the students.
(iv) Promotion of cultural heritage by broadening the outlook of students.
(v) Involvement of students in community service and welfare activities.
(vi) Development of ideals and values of emotional integration and national unity.
(vii) Development of social awareness.
(viii) Development of values of secularism, socialism and democracy.

CHARACTERISTICS OF THE PROCESS OF EDUCATION

1. *Education. A Tripolar and Multipolar Process*: Education is also regarded as a tripolar process involving the interaction of the personality of the educator on that of the educand in a social setting which affects the modification of the behaviour of the educand. The knowledge of the nature of the educand is at once very useful and essential. Similarly the educator also must thoroughly understand himself—his assets and limitations and act accordingly in educating the educand. The social setting has to be presented by the educator to the educand in a simplified and purified manner. It must be remembered that the unconscious influence of the environment is subtle and pervasive.

The basic system of education as propounded by Gandhi emphasised three aspects (a) the student, (b) the craft, and (c) the environment—physical and social. Introducing the third element, i.e. the social environment. Dewey has emphasised the society as the source of the curriculum or subjects to be taught. Since all these three poles—the teacher, the pupil and curriculum are important, education is called a tripolar process.

2. *Education. A Deliberate Process*: The process of education is not only conscious but also deliberate. The educator is fully aware of the fact that his aim is to develop the personality of the child along definite lines through the modification of his behaviour.

3. *Education. A Sociological Process*: This implies that the educator must interpret and develop the endowments (capacities) of the child in a social setting. A child is a social being and as such must be educated in such a way that he becomes a useful member of the society.

4. *Education. A Psychological Process*: According to the psychological aspect of the process, the educator must understand the nature, interests, capacities and limitations of the child.

5. *Education. A Child-centred Process*: The modern educator considers the child as a 'hero' in the drama of education and assigns the central place to him. The subject-matter, the teacher and the environment are all for him and not he for them. The child-centred process signifies that the educator must study each child carefully and attend to his individual needs. Since the child is the focus, the school curriculum and environment must provide for his total growth taking into account all the essential areas: the aesthetic, the creative, the ethical, the linguistic, the manual, the mathematical, the physical, the scientific, the social and the spiritual.

6. *Education. A Life Long Process*: Education is a cradle-to-the-grave process, no longer a concentration on the early years. Every year, every month, every day and every minute, step by step a person learns. In the new world no one knows what the morrow will bring. And so every individual must equip

himself in every moment of his life to meet the new challenges in life. Education at all stages must become self-education, so that with the tools of education acquired at school, the adult will continue his education throughout life with all the means at his disposal—the library, the reading room, camps, tours, mass media, clubs, institutions, etc. Life long education is acquired through formal, non-formal and informal means of education.

WHY, WHOM, WHO, WHERE, WHAT, HOW AND WHEN OF EDUCATION

1. *Why to Educate*? This includes aims of education. The educator and the educand must be clear about the aims of education so that efforts are made in the right direction. Aims of education depend upon a host of factors: political, economic, social, geographical, religious etc. In a nutshell, education must produce socially efficient individuals.

2. *Whom to Educate*? The educator must understand the educand, i.e., the child thoroughly—his aptitude, interest, temperaments etc. so that the 'best of him' is 'drawn out'.

3. *Who is to Educate*? The teacher is to educate and he must thoroughly understand himself also. He must rid himself of all the blemishes and remember 'Woe to the teacher who teaches one thing with the lips and carries another in the heart'.

4. *Where to Educate*? The child is to be educated in a school which must 'simplify', 'purify' and 'idealise' the environment. Likewise there are several other agencies that supplement school's work.

5. *What to Educate*? This leads to the contents of the curriculum which has been described as 'the environment in motion'. In a broader sense it includes all the courses, readings, associations and activities that go in the school—in the classroom, library, laboratory, workshop, playgrounds and in the numerous informal contacts between teachers and pupils.

6. *How to Educate*? This involves the knowledge and technique of various methods of teaching for making the

teaching-learning process dynamic, effective and inspirational.

7. *When to Educate*? This is concerned with the different stages of the child so that 'motivational' aspects may be handled and attended to psychologically.

SCOPE OF EDUCATION

Scope of education is as vast as life itself. There is no aspect or dimension of life which is not covered under education. In fact all education is life and all life is education. Education is a life-long process. Education is formal, non-formal and informal. Likewise agencies of education are formal, non-formal and informal.

Every year, every month, every day, every moment, step by step we learn from every source.

Education is concerned with the aesthetic, cultural, ethical, intellectual, physical, religious, social, spiritual and vocational development of the individual.

Education has moved away from preparing pupils to fit into a particular society but it seeks to make them feel they belong to the larger world family.

2

Types of Education

THREE TYPES OF EDUCATION

Broadly speaking, there are three types of education although with the development of ICT (Information Communication Technology), the difference among these has been declining.

Three types of education are as under:

1. Formal Education
2. Informal Education
3. Non-formal Education

FORMAL EDUCATION

Formal education is imparted in an educational institution—a school or college. In ancient time in India, it was mostly imparted at the residence of the teacher. It is consciously and deliberately planned to bring about specific changes in the educand or the learner. As such it is synonymous with educational institutions. School is the most important agency of formal education.

Important characteristics of formal education are:

1. Planned education keeping in view some definite aim.
2. Education imparted through well-planned means or formal lessons.
3. Education having a definite course to be covered during a definite period.

4. A teaching-learning process with which the teacher and the learner are acquainted.
5. Education organised by some agency, say the Government or the private enterprise.
6. Education imparted in an institution having building/ premises.
7. Education starting and ending at a particular age.
8. Education associated with a degree or certificate.
9. Education usually associated with some sort of mental strain on the teacher and the taught.

INFORMAL EDUCATION

Informal education takes into its orbit all indirect influences of the home and the society. The press, the libraries, the films and other such agencies are included as agencies of informal education. Their influence is subtle and imperceptible but at the same time very important and significant.

Important characteristics of informal education are:

1. Unconscious learning.
2. No fixed aim.
3. No fixed curriculum or methods of teaching etc.
4. No organised body or institution behind this process.
5. Life-long learning.
6. Natural outcome.

NON-FORMAL EDUCATION

This is an arrangement wherein flexibility is the key word. The system is an open one with regards to various aspects of education, i.e., admissions, curriculum, place of instruction, mode of instruction and the time and duration of instruction. Open university, open learning, the correspondence courses and distant education are the various examples of such a system.

Important characteristics of non-formal education are:

1. Flexibility in various aspects of education, i.e., admissions, place of education, curriculum, age, co-curricular activities, modes of teaching, evaluation etc.
2. Covering life span of an individual.
3. Guided by motivation of the individual for self-growth, self-renewal.
4. Diversified curriculum responsive to learner and environmental needs.
5. Process of sharing, exploring, analysing and judging with maximum participation of the learner.
6. Preparation for future needs.
7. Part-time education.

Some of the important definitions of non-formal education are:

1. *Bremwork*: "Non-formal education differs from formal education from the point of proximity to immediate action, work and the opportunity to put learning to use".
2. *Coombs*: "Non-formal education is one which is imparted through organisations and institutions outside the formal education institutions."
3. *Harbison*: "Non-formal education is the only means of filling the gap between the 'Schooled' and 'Unschooled population'."
4. *Henderson*: "Non formal education is far wider and more inclusive than schooling which imparts wider experience out of school".
5. *Mc-Call*: "Non-formal education is the entire range of learning experience outside the regular graded school system".
6. *Paulson*: "Non-formal education includes any structured, systematic, non-school educational and training activities of relatively short duration in which

sponsoring agencies seek concrete behavioural changes in fairly distinct target population."

Main Characteristics of Non-formal Education

1. *Learner Centred-Education*: It is based on the needs of the learners.
2. *Life-long-Process*: It continues throughout life.
3. *Self-Education*: There is more emphasis on self-education.
4. *Boom for Drop-outs*: It provides suitable opportunities to those who on account of one or the other reason are unable to continue their formal education.
5. *Motivational*: It is motivated by individual growth.
6. *Community Need Based*: It takes note of the needs of the community and accordingly includes a variety of learning programmes.
7. *No Formal Qualifications Needed*: A large number of non-formal educational courses do not need minimum qualifications for entry.
8. *Multi-dimensional*: It provides a variety of opportunities to update one's knowledge and skills.
9. *Supplementary to Formal Education*: It supplements the system of formal education which is rather expensive.
10. *Multi-Agencies*: It is provided by part-time schools, open schools, adult education centres and voluntary agencies.
11. *Flexible System*: It is flexible in terms of hours of study, courses, examinations, duration, etc.

NON-FORMAL EDUCATION AND NATIONAL POLICY ON EDUCATION—NPE (1986 AND REVISED POLICY 1992)

The NPE has assigned an important place to non-formal education at the elementary stage of education and adult education. The programme of Non-formal education as envisaged in the policy in Part 5 is given below:

5.8 (*Revised Para*) *The Non-formal Education Programme, meant for school drop-outs, for children from habitations without schools, working children and girls who cannot attend whole day schools, will be strengthened and enlarged.*

5.8 (NPE, 1986) A large and systematic programme of non-formal education will be launched for school drop-outs, for children, from habitations without schools, working children and girls who cannot attend whole day schools.

5.9 (Revised Para) Modern technological aids will be used to improve the learning environment of NFE Centres. Talented and dedicated young men and women from the local community will be chosen to serve as instructors, and particular attention paid to their training. All necessary measures will be taken to ensure that the quality of non-formal education is comparable with the formal education. Steps will be taken to facilitate lateral entry into the formal system of children passing out of the non-formal system.

5.9 (NPE, 1986) Modern technological aids will be used to improve the learning environment of NFE centres. Talented and dedicated young men and women from the local community will be chosen to serve as instructors, and particular attention paid to their training. Steps will be taken to facilitate their entry into the formal system in deserving cases. All necessary measures will be taken to ensure that the quality of non-formal education is comparable with formal education.

5.10 Effective steps will be taken to provide a framework for the curriculum on the lines of the national core curriculum, but based on the needs of the learners and related to the local environment. Learning material of high quality will be developed and provided free of charge to all pupils. NFE programmes will provide participatory learning environment, and activities, such as, games and sports, cultural programmes, excursions, etc.

5.11 (*Revised Para*) *The Government will take overall responsibility for this vital sector. Voluntary agencies and Panchayati Raj institutions will take much of the responsibility of running NFE programmes. The provision of funds to these agencies will be adequate and timely.*

5.11 (NPE, 1986) Much of the work running of NFE centers will be done through voluntary agencies and panchayati raj institutions. The provision of funds to the agencies will be adequate and timely. The Government will take overall responsibility for this vital sector.

BROAD COMPARISON BETWEEN FORMAL AND NON-FORMAL EDUCATION

	Area	*Formal Education*	*Non-Formal Education*
1.	*Aims*	1. All-round development 2. To get a certificate or degree needed for a job or self-employment	(i) To increase knowledge and skills. (ii) To better qualifications. (iii) To pursue studies for self-satisfaction.
2.	*Place*	An educational institution – school or college – full time.	No specific place is important to learners – can be home, factory, farm, library, open space, etc.
3.	*Learners*	It caters to learners who are in a position to attend full time.	It caters to learners who cannot go to school or have dropped. It also includes learners who want to improve their qualifications by studying at home.
4.	*Age*	Usually prescribed ages.	Any age.
5.	*Grade*	Students are grouped into classes.	Usually no grouping.
6.	*Curriculum*	Rigid and fixed.	Curriculum not fixed.
7.	*Textbooks*	Prescribed textbooks	Usually no prescribed text-books.
8.	*Examination*	Examination at regular intervals. Written tests. Essay and short answer-questions.	Normally no examination. Assignments.

(Contd.)

	Area	*Formal Education*	*Non-Formal Education*
9.	*Teachers*	Several teachers on full time basis.	Usually part time teachers.
10.	*Methods of Teaching*	Direct teaching methods, Face to face teaching, Lecturing.	Contact programmes, radio, T.V. Correspondence lesson, very little face to face teaching.
12.	*Period*	It is limited to a period of 'being taught' as against a period of 'life' and 'work'. It is imparted in educational institutions.	It is lifelong with learning integrated with life and work. Life is upgraded and enriched by learning.
13.	*Points of Entry*	It has fixed points of entry and exit. Age of admission and entry qualifications are prescribed.	It has flexible points of entry and exist, re-entry and re-exit and so on throughout the life span of the individual.
14.	*Employment Function*	It is employment-oriented.	It is motivated by individual growth, self-renewal and maximising human potential.
15.	*Interaction*	It is usually imposed by 'giver' on the 'receiver' with little interaction between the two.	It is expected to be a process of sharing, exploring, analysing and judging together with participation of the learner.
16.	*Freedom*	It usually fosters an uncritical command obedience.	It develops an open-end critical and self-reliant awareness.
17.	*Access*	It works on the principle of weeding out 'failures'.	It works on the principle or universal success through universal learning satisfaction.
18.	*Status Quo*	It nurtures the status quo and discourages deviation.	It encourages healthy points of departure towards progress.

(*Contd.*)

	Area	*Formal Education*	*Non-Formal Education*
19.	*Social Frame Work*	It works within a fixed social frame and hence gets quickly out of step with social change.	It anticipates and prepares for change for the future.
20.	*Environment*	Specially created environment.	Normal Environment.
21.	*Agencies*	Usually full time institutions. They are well-organised.	Usually part time agencies. They are not well-organised.
22.	*Rules and Regulations*	Rules and regulations are usually rigid.	Rules and regulations are usually flexible.

COMPARISON OF FORMAL AND INFORMAL EDUCATION

	Area	*Formal Education*	*Informal Education*
1.	*Objective*	There is some defi-nite objective to be achieved.	There may or may not be any objective to be achieved.
2.	*Place of Study*	It is imparted in an institution.	There is no definite place. Even the home of the indivi-dual student may take the place of education.
3.	*Planning*	It is planned.	It has no definite planning.
4.	*Nature of Course*	There is a definite course to be covered during a definite period.	There is no such definite course and period.
5.	*Type of Lessons*	It is imparted through formal lessons or well-planned means.	It is not imparted through any formal lesson or well-planned means.
6.	*Awareness of the Process*	Both the teacher and the taught are aware of the process through which education is imparted.	The teacher and the taught are not conscious of the process.

(*Contd.*)

Area	Formal Education	Informal Education
7. *Age*	It starts and ends at a particular age.	There is no age bar.
8. *Mental Strain*	It puts mental strain both on the teacher and the taught.	Being natural, does not put strain or anybody.
9. *Organisation*	It is organised by some agency—say the Government or non-governmental institutions.	There may not be any such organisation for the organisation of this type of education.
10. *Evaluation*	Work of the learner is evaluated from time to time.	There is no evaluation.
11. *Nature of Contact*	Normally teaching is done face to face.	Education may not be face to face.
12. *Qualification of Teachers*	Persons who impart training are themselves trained.	No training is needed.
13. *Time Schedule*	There is a fixed time-table to be followed.	No fixed time-table is followed.
14. *Rules and Regulations*	There are definite rules and regulations.	There are no rules and regulations.
15. *Degree or Diplomas*	It involves granting of a degree or diploma.	No degree or diploma is awarded.
16. *Discipline*	Students are expected to observe a definite type of discipline.	There is no such requirement.
17. *Period of Schooling/Stages/Classes*	Period of Schooling is fixed	It is a life long process. It has neither any end nor beginning. It continues for the whole life.

COMPARISON AMONG FORMAL, INFORMAL AND NON-FORMAL EDUCATION

Area	Formal Education	Informal Education	Non-formal Education
1. *Aim*	It has definite aims.	It has no definite aim.	It has mostly clear-cut aims.

(*Contd.*

Area	*Formal Education*	*Informal Education*	*Non-formal Education*
2. *Scope*	Its scope is definite.	Its scope is not definite.	Its scope is generally definite.
3. *Duration*	It begins from school and goes up to university.	It is life long.	It can be life-long.
4. *Entry Points*	It has fixed entry points.	It has no entry point.	Entry points are flexible.
5. *Agencies*	It is provided usually in full time educational institutions.	It has no definite agencies.	It is normally available through part time institutions.
6. *Organisation*	It is an organised and planned effort. There is usually a recognised organisation, which is more or less permanent.	There is no organisation for it.	Organisation may not be a permanent one. Ad-hoc organisations usually take up this work.
7. *Time Schedule*	Its schedule is fixed.	It has no fixed schedule.	Schedule fixed as well as not fixed.
8. *Conscious*	The teacher and the learners are aware of the process.	Unconscious process.	It is partly conscious.
9. *Methodology*	Format, fixed and a variety of methods.	There is no set methodology.	Flexible approach is followed.
10. *Teachers*	Trained teachers impart education.	It can be obtained from any source.	Trained teachers/ instructors impart non-formal education.
11. *Place*	It is confined to the four walls of educational institutions.	It can be acquired at any place.	It mostly takes place outside the four walls of educational institutes.

(*Contd.*)

Area	*Formal Education*	*Informal Education*	*Non-formal Education*
12. *Environment*	Environment is more or less artificial.	Environment is natural.	Environment is artificial as well as natural.
13. *Curriculum*	Curriculum is fixed.	There is no curriculum.	Curriculum is very flexible.
14. *Discipline*	Discipline is normally strict.	Issue of discipline does not exist.	Discipline is rather flexible.
15. *Resources Required*	Relatively higher resources are needed.	Resources are not needed.	Comparatively less resources are required.
16. *Evaluation and Examination*	Examination are regularly held.	There is no examination.	Examination are not frequent.
17. *Award of Certificates and Degrees*	Certificate and degrees form an integral part.	Certificate/degree is not given or received.	Certificate or degree may or may not be awarded.
18. *Mental Stress*	It involves lot of mental stress.	No mental strain is involved.	Usually no mental strain is involved.
19. *Motivation*	The teachers and learners are motivated.	Motivation is not involved.	Normally motivation on the part of the learners is quite high.
20. *Interaction*	There is face to face interaction which is quite visible.	Interaction is incidental.	Interaction depends upon the situation.
21. *Pass/Failure*	Students are labelled 'passed' or 'failure'.	Pass/Failure does not exist.	Normally it does not work on the principle of wee-ding, not failures.
22. *Planning*	It is a planned system.	No planning is required.	Planning is flexible.

EXAMPLES OF DIFFERENT TYPES OF EDUCATION

	Types of Education	*Examples*
1.	Formal Education	School, College
2.	Non-formal	Radio, TV, Press etc.
3.	Informal	Social gatherings. Entire environment. Unconscious learning. Through imitation. Sitting on the table within a group. Street and market place.

NARROWING DOWN THE GAP BETWEEN DIFFERENT TYPES OF EDUCATION

The revolution in information and communication technology (ICT) and its use in the teaching-learning process has narrowed down the difference. The use of computers, radio and TV has introduced several elements of formal education into informal and non-formal education and vice versa. At one time radio and TV were used only for the purpose of non-formal education. Now they are being used in a planned way for formal education. In fact there is a special TV channel for this purpose. It is estimated that at the higher education level, nearly 10 per cent enrolment is through Distance Education/Open Education. New Slogans like 'Open Learning', 'University Without Walls', and 'Virtual University' are taking the place of formal education which at one time was confined to the 'four walls' of the school/college. Use of Internet for educational purposes has become very popular. CDs on different subjects are available now. Students have the opportunities of pursuing their studies in their bedrooms. They can get University Degrees without visiting any place or even without coming into personal contact with the teachers. Students can complete their degrees without any prescribed schedule.

A BALANCED VIEW

We should try to avert the danger of education being isolated from the subject-matter of life experience. Hence one of the weightiest problems with which the philosophy of education has to cope with is of keeping a proper balance between the informal and the formal and the non-formal modes of education. Hence we should try to incorporate the good points of non-informal education as far as we can. The formal education makes it easier to bridge the gulf between the immature nature of the child and the demands of the society. The non-formal education helps to bridge the gulf between the education imparted in the school and the education needed to lead a successful life as a member of the community.

TRADITIONAL EDUCATION AND MODERN EDUCATION AT A GLANCE

Aspect	*Traditional Education*	*Modern Education*
1. *Aim*	Knowledge of 3 R's—Reading, Writing and Arithmetic, i.e., knowledge of subjects.	1. Training in 7 R's, i.e. Reading, Writing and Arithmetic, i.e., Teaching of subjects, Rights, Responsibilities and Relationship. 2. Development of total personality. 3. Social efficiency.
2. *Function*	Broadly religious	Broadly social
3. *Contents/Curriculum*	Subjectscentred	Subjects and experiences
4. *Agencies*	Family, school and church etc.	School, several agencies, mass media.
5. *Teacher*	Autocrat, policeman	Democrat, humanist.
6. *School*	A Place for the pouring in of knowledge	1. Place for training in citizenship and democracy. Art of living together.

(*Contd.*)

Aspect	Traditional Education	Modern Education
		2. Idealised miniature society.
7. *Child*	Like dumb-driven cattle, passive.	Human being. Active.
8. *Individual differences*	Not recognised.	Utmost consideration to individual differences.
9. *Methods of teaching.*	Bookish, memorisation, mechaniccal.	Dynamic and challenging. Question answer. Project method, Discovery method, etc.
10. *Courses*	Usually single track.	Diversified
11. *Life experiences*	Very few	Related to life.
12. *Media*	Mainly chalk and board.	New Media also.
13. *Discipline*	Rule of the 'rod'	Self and social discipline.
14. *Examination*	Rigid. Essay type.	Comprehensive and continuous, objective, tests, etc.
15. *Chief concern*	Religious and spiritual	1. Sociological.
		2. Several new concerns like environmental education and population education, etc.
		3. New technologies.

EMERGING CONCERNS AND MODERN EDUCATION

The world has never changed so rapidly as in recent years. Eminent thinkers in the world began to contemplate in the 1990s on the emerging modern society and its impact on the modern education. UNESCO took the lead and in 1993 appointed an International Commission on Education for the 21st Century to consider the various dimensions of modern education. The Commission gave its report in 1996.

Major Issues Confronting the Society and Consequently Education

According to the Commission, modern education must take note of the following:

1. Tension between the global and local situations.
2. Tension between the universal and the individual.
3. Tension between tradition and modernity.
4. Tension between long term and short term considerations.
5. Tension, on the one hand the need for competition and on the other, concern for equality of opportunity.
6. Tension between the extraordinary expansion of knowledge and human beings capacity to assimilate it.
7. Tension between the spiritual and the material.

CHILD-CENTRED EDUCATION AND TEACHER-CENTRED EDUCATION

Dimensions	*Child-Centred Education*	*Teacher-Centred Education*
1. Goals	Goals set by the learner with assistance and the guidance by the teacher to meet the diverse needs as they evolve.	Goals set by the teacher in advance to meet the needs that he has anticipated.
2. Approach	Discovery and experience approach to learning. Situations and resources provided by the teacher for the learner to generate, experience and discover ideas for himself.	Information and ideas put over to the child by the teacher.

(*Contd.*)

	Dimensions	Child-Centred Education	Teacher-Centred Education
3.	Homogeneity	Wide variety of activeties at any one time. Various learners doing different activeties suiting their needs at that point of time.	Same learning experiences for all students at any one time. All learners attend the same sessions and do the same things.
4.	Sequencing	Very flexible sequence. Sequence not determined in advance but according to the felt need of the learner. Similar items may be learned in different sequences by different learners.	Sequences or order fixed in advance. Sequences are determined according to the preferences of the teacher.
5.	Control	Decisions made by learners or jointly by the learners and the teacher. Hence joint control over the course.	Decisions made by the teacher and he maintains control over the course.
6.	Method	Wide variety of learning-teaching methods. Methods usually selected by the learners.	Relatively few teaching-learning methods. Methods selected by the teachers.
7.	Learner tutor relationship.	Very close, open, personal relationship.	Distant. Closed. Formal relationship.
8.	Group attitude	Trusting, supportive. Close relationships.	Not quite trusting. Not very supportive. Learners relatively distant from each other.
9.	Feelings	Full expression	Very restricted expression of feelings.
10.	Discipline	Free. Full of freedom.	Strict. Do's and Don'ts.

3

Aims and Objectives of Education

AIMS OF EDUCATION RELATED TO SOCIETY

A.K.C. Ottaway has rightly stated, "Education is an activity which goes on in a society and its aims and methods depend on the nature of the society in which it takes place". Likewise Clark has observed, "No writer on education, however, much he may strive after universality of thought can wholly shake himself free from the influence of time and space".

Aims are related to real situations of life. Education to be effective must meet the many-sided needs of the society. A child is not to be educated in a vacuum. He is a member of the society in which he lives and education must help him to become a useful member of that society.

Since, economic, physical, political, religious and social needs differ from place to place, from time to time and country to country, the educational aims also differ.

1. *Economic Factors*: Formal education is possible where production exceeds consumption. This may be the result of tremendous industrial development or favourable natural circumstances. This will depend upon fertility of soil, abundant mineral deposits and proper climatic conditions for work. Such conditions provide men with leisure to pursue education. Where there is a subsistence economy, it is a far cry to afford time for formal schooling. This is the reason why poorer and undeveloped countries have a minimum education for their children while industrially advanced countries afford to keep nearly all their children at school and for a longer time.

2. *Geographical Factors*: Educational system in ancient Greek States presents an interesting study. Education in Sparta aimed at developing physical strength, courage and endurance and obedience because the immediate aim was to train the Spartan youth as soldiers who could protect the state from foreign aggression. Athian education on the other hand was finer.

3. *Political Factors*: Political ideologies go a long way in determining the aims and the system of education. Different political ideologies like egalitarian or fascist communist or socialist and democratic will call for different systems of education.

The ruled nations had a different educational system than their rulers as they were being exploited by their rulers. The system of British education was implanted in this country from purely political motives.

4. *Religious Factors*: The influence of religion is very powerful as it penetrates the emotional depth of human nature. The Brahmanic system of education, the Buddhist education and the early Mohammedan education were dominated by religion. Similarly in Europe, the Protestant countries were wedded to the education of the masses and the Catholic countries to the education of the classes.

5. *Social Factors*: Education reflects the social pattern of society. The tremendous explosion of science and technology has shaken the old leisurely outlook on life and has created intricate problems of social adjustment. A new emphasis has been placed on literacy. A growing interest is shown in reorganising the curricula at all stages. The new forces in the social structure of the Indian society have provided a fresh incentive for educationists to pattern the educational system.

Aim of Education in Primitive Societies

In ancient times men needed training in the use of bows and arrows for their safety. Their needs were simple and few. The process of production, consumption, distribution and exchange was quite simple. Thus, the educative needs were also simple and these could be met by a process of education which was also very simple.

Aim of Education in a Totalitarian State

The aims of education are determined by the political ideologies. J.F. Brown says, "Education in any country and at all periods reflects ideologies of the ruling class". There are many instances in the history of the world when persons with different ideologies from their rulers were threatened, sacked, and even assassinated. In Russia, the individual was to be trained in a way so as to become a Communist, in Germany a Nationalist Socialist and in Italy a Fascist. The aim of education is to force upon every individual an ideology which he must not question. The creed will be reflected in the curriculum, syllabi, methods, and techniques of education.

Aim of Education in Ancient India

Education in ancient India was in the hands of the Brahmans, and religion played an important role in the life of an individual. Indian education aimed at inculcating a spirit of piety and righteousness. Education constituted a real training for living life according to spiritual and moral values.

Aim of Education in Medieval India

The aim was religious and the educator was required to produce pious and religious minded people. Maktabs and Madarsas were the places where education was imparted. These institutions were generally run in mosques.

Aims of Education in British India

There was a radical change in the aims of education with the advent of British rule in India. Lord Macaulay laid down the aims of education in the Famous Minutes of 1835. The aim of the educational system was to train an army of individuals who could assist the Britishers in the administration of this country. Macaulay wanted an educational system which might bring about the cultural conquest of the people of India by the British.

Aims of Education in Free India

The ideals and values embodied in the Preamble to the Constitution of India are the guiding sources of educational aims in India. These may be expressed as under:

1. Development of democratic values.
2. Development of egalitarian values.
3. Development of secular values.
4. Development of values related to dignity of individual.
5. Development of values conducive to the unity of the country.
6. Development of the capacity of the individual to earn his livelihood.
7. Development of the capacity of an individual to increase national product.

General Aims of Education

1. Aesthetic aim.
2. Complete living aim.
3. Cultural aim.
4. Harmonious and all-round development aim.
5. Happiness aim.
6. Individual aim.
7. International understanding aim.
8. Knowledge aim.
9. Leisure aim.
10. Moral aim.
11. Physical health and well-being aim.
12. Political aim.
13. Religious aim.
14. Self-realisation aim.
15. Social aim.
16. Spiritual aim.
17. Vocational aim.

Summing up: Education to be effective cannot have a single aim. An ideal balance among various aims has to be struck.

INDIVIDUAL AIM AND SOCIAL AIM OF EDUCATION

Individual Aim of Education

The individual aim in education has found support from the following:

1. *Individual Aim and the Biologists*: Prof. G. Thompson has observed, "Education is for the individual: its function being to enable the individual to survive and live out his complete life".

2. *Individual Aim and the Naturalists*: In the words of Rousseau, the most ardent supporter of the individual aim in education, "Everything is good as it comes from the hands of the Author of Nature". Accordingly, he and others who also think likewise advocate that education should be in accordance with the nature of the individual.

3. *Individual Aim and the Psychologists*: According to psychologists, each individual is a unique one and accordingly education should develop the innate powers of the individual.

4. *Individual Aim and the Spiritualists*: The Spiritualists are of the view that every individual is a separate identity and responsible for his own actions. Therefore, the main aim of education is to lead the individual to his self-satisfaction.

Criticism of the Individual Aim of Education

1. The critics of individual aim believe that the individual left to himself will be selfish and indisciplined. The animal instinct of man, if given, a loose region is sure to lead him to the state of primitive barbarism where the law of jungle prevailed.

2. The exaggerated claim of the individual may have an adverse effect in the politics and economy of a country. The policy of *Laissezfaire* is not conducive to national interests in the modern times.

3. Absolute freedom to the individual should not be given. The individual may begin to assert that I must have what I want.

4. According to Raymont, an individual is only a figment of imagination. An individual cannot be conceived in isolation from society.

Supporters of Social Aim of Education

1. Gandhiji formulated the basic scheme with the objective of making people realise that education was not merely for the benefit of the individual but for the needs of a predominantly rural and agrarian population.

2. According to John Dewey, social aim in education is stressed as education should make each individual socially efficient, and this social efficiency must be achieved by the positive use of individual powers and capacities in social occupations. A socially efficient individual is not a drag or parasite on society or any individual. A socially efficient individual is able to earn his livelihood. He also conforms to moral and social standards of conduct.

3. Raymont says that the isolated individual is "a figment of the imagination". The individual being a social animal, will be moulded to the needs of the society. The individual will develop through social contacts.

4. According to the Education Commission 1964-66, "Education cannot be considered in isolation or planned in a vacuum. It has to be used as a powerful instrument of a social, economic and political change and will, therefore, have to be related to the long-term national aspirations, the programmes of National Development in which the country is engaged and the difficult short-term problem it is called upon to face".

Limitations of Social Aims of Education

1. Social aim of education envisages the individual as a non-entity and leaves little scope for his personality development.
2. Extreme form of social aim has led to the concept. "My country! Wrong or right" This emphasis became

responsible for the rise of Nazism in Germany and Fascism in Italy. As a result of this, Second World War took place.

3. Undue stress on social aim of education is against the concept of universal brotherhood.

Synthesis between Individual and Social Aim of Education

The individual and the society, both be regarded as realities. Neither of the two is absolutely independent of the other. Instead of being regarded as isolated entities, the individual and the society should be considered as functionally related to each other – the individual acting on the society, and the society reacting on the individual. The individual is the product of society which the society in its own turn finds its advancement in the development of its individual members. In the words of John Adam, 'Individuality requires a social medium to grow. Without social contacts we are not human."

According to Ross, "Individuality is of no value and personality is a meaningless term apart from the social environment in which they are developed and made manifest". Self-realisation can be achieved only through social service and social ideas of real value can come into being only through free individuals who have developed valuable individuality. The circle cannot be broken.

PRIORITIES OF AIMS OF EDUCATION IN INDIA

Aims of Education in Accordance with the Nature of Indian Society

The Indian Constitution with its statements contained in the Preamble, Fundamental Rights and Directive Principles form the chief sources of aim of education in India.

The goals placed before the people by the Constitution are those of a democratic society which recognises the dignity and the basic rights of the individual and holds the promise of an order in which social, political and economic justice and equality will prevail.

The salient features of the Indian society as envisaged in the Constitution are:

1. Indian society must be based on the principles of secularism, socialism and democracy.
2. Indian society must be based on justice: social, economic and social.
3. Indian society must provide for liberty of thought, expression, belief, faith and worship.
4. Indian society must be based on equality of status and opportunity.
5. Indian society must be based on fraternity, assuring the dignity of the individual and the unity of the nation.
6. Indian society must provide a reasonable standard of living to its members.

Brief History of Aims of Education in India

As stated from time to time the first attempt to list aims of education in India was made by the University Education Commission (1948-49). The aims were confined to higher education only. Besides, these were formulated before the commencement of Indian Constitution. The second attempt was made by the Secondary Education Commission (1952-53). These related to secondary education only.

The Education Commission (1964-66), popularly known as the Kothari Commission went into reforms of all aspects of education including aims of education.

The Education Commission suggested the following aims of education:

1. Vocational aim for increasing productivity.
2. Character development, i.e., development of moral, social and spiritual values.
3. National and emotional integration aim.
4. Democratic aim.
5. Modernisation of Indian society through awakening of curiosity.

Character Development Aim of Education

A man of character is bound to be liberal, appreciative of his duties and responsibilities towards himself and the society and to remain above the sectarian, regional and religious considerations. He follows the values of secularism, socialism and democracy. Therefore, character formation is the first aim of education in India.

Character has two facets: the one which is personal, and the other which manifests itself in our relationship with society. Both these aspects should be pure and unsullied.

Gandhiji has observed, "All our learning or recitation of the Vedas, correct knowledge of Sanskrit, Latin, Greek and what not will avail us nothing if they do not enable us to cultivate absolute purity of heart. The end of all knowledge must be building up of character". Raymount states, "The teacher's ultimate concern is to cultivate, not wealth of muscle, nor fullness of knowledge, nor refinement of feeling, but strength and purity of character". According to Vivekanand, "The end of all education, all training should be man making". John Dewey has said, "All education forms character–mental and moral". The Secondary Education Commission has observed, "Education is the training of character to fit the students to participate creatively as citizens".

Character is the product of daily, hourly actions and words and thoughts; daily forgiveness, unselfishness, kindness, sympathies, charities; sacrifices for the good of others, struggles against temptations. What is character without elementary personal purity?

In India today we find a lack of character at various levels so much so that the actions of the VIP's also create doubts in the mind of the common man. State of affairs is very shocking. The present saying is: 'As the ruler, so the people'. Perhaps after independence, morality or character has been the greatest causality. Education, therefore, must be devoted to character building activities.

Vocational Aim of Education

Moral or character formation aim of education is also one-sided. An individual must be prepared to earn his livelihood otherwise he will not be a happy man. Of course, values of life must not be sacrificed for "bread and butter".

Gandhiji has also supported the vocational aim. He observed, "True education ought to be for them (boys and girls) a kind of insurance against unemployment". The vocational aim is also called the "bread and butter aim". It can train individuals to become socially efficient. They will, therefore, neither be drags nor parasites on the society. They will contribute to increase production and national wealth. The advocates of the vocational aim argue that all the knowledge a pupil gains in the school, all the culture the pupil acquires in the school will be of no use, if he cannot make both ends meet when he enters life.

Synthesis of Character Formation and Vocational Aim of Education

Vocational aim in education has its own importance but man does not live by bread alone. Education must take into consideration the entire personality of the pupil and not one segment of it. Man has to develop himself aesthetically, intellectually, morally, physically and socially. The University Education Commission 1948-1949 has very rightly observed, "If we wish to bring about a savage upheaval in our society, a *Rakshas Raj*, all that we need to do is to give vocational and technical education to starve the spirit. We will have number of scientists without conscience, technicians without taste, who find a void within themselves a moral vacuum and a desperate need to substitute something, anything for their lost endeavour and purpose".

Pt. Nehru has stated, "Education has mainly two aspects, the cultural aspect which makes a person grow, and the productive aspect which makes a person do things. Both are essential. Everybody should be a producer as well as a good citizen and not a sponge on another person even though the other person may be one's own husband or wife". Gandhiji, it is true, stressed the vocational aspect but at the same time he was very emphatic, "By education, I mean an all-round drawing out of the best in child and man-body, mind and spirit". He was convinced that without character, vocational efficiency had no meaning.

FUNCTIONS AND DIRECTIONS OF EDUCATION IN INDIA

General Functions of Education in Life. Education is expected to perform the following functions:

1. Development of natural abilities of individuals.
2. Development of such capacities in the individuals that help them to harness the natural resources of the country.
3. Development of character.
4. Development of personality.
5. Preparation for living present life.
6. Preparation for adult life and future life.
7. Sublimation of instincts.
8. Creation of socially efficient individuals.
9. Development of community sense.
10. Conservation and promotion of culture and civilisation.
11. Involvement in social welfare.
12. National development.
13. Development of suitable leisure time activities.
14. Developing values of emotional integration.
15. Developing universal brotherhood.

Factors Influencing Functions and Directions of Education in India

As already observed, educational systems is to be transformed in such a way as it fully meets the requirements of a society as envisaged in the Constitution of India. Among the important characteristics of the Indian society are to be (i) Democratic, (ii) Socialist, (iii) Secular, (iv) Modern. Inherent in these are the concept of a welfare state, i.e., raising the standard of living can be improved only with increased production and equitable distribution of wealth. All this demands that education in India should be geared to perform the functions as discussed here.

1. *Social Development*: An individual is social by nature. He always resides and works in society. He has to live and act in the society as a social being. Education, therefore, must aim at social development. The social development finds expression in such concepts as 'education for social service' and 'education for social efficiency'.

2. *Education for Human Resource Development*: The Education Commission 1964-66 has described the situation as "There can be no hope of making the country self- sufficient in food unless the farmer himself is moved out of his age-long conservation through a science-based education, becomes interested in experimentation, and is ready to adopt techniques that increase production. The same is true of industry. The skilled manpower needed for the relevant research and its systematic application to agriculture, industry and other sectors of life can only come from a development of scientific and technological education. Similarly, economic growth is not merely a matter of physical resources or of training skilled workers, it needs the education of the whole population in new ways of life, thought and work".

3. *The Development of Physical Resources of the Country*: This can be made possible through the modernisation of agriculture and rapid industrialisation. This requires the adoption of a science-based technology, heavy capital formation and investment and the provision of the essential infrastructure of transport, credit, marketing and other institutions.

4. *Education for the Development of Skills*: Our principal potential asset is our people. Whether using a plough, driving a truck, designing a steel mill or typing business letters, the human factor is common and vital to all branches of economics activity. Education has an essential role to play in the structure and effectiveness of the country's work force. Education is

indispensable in all occupations as it develops proper insight. As economic and productive activities expand there is a greater need for educated people to design, plan, supervise, manufacture, sell and administer. Services of all kinds grow in step with industry. All services need educated personnel for operation and administration.

5. *Education Ensuring Equality of Opportunity*: The National Policy on Education, 1986 has observed, "the New Policy will lay special emphasis on the removal of disparities and to equalise educational opportunity by attending to the specific needs of those who have been denied equality so far".

6. *Democratisation of Education and the Involvement of People*: Democratising education does not only mean giving more education to more people, but also involving more people in educational management.

7. *Meeting the Needs of an Egalitarian Society*: Education should develop such attitudes and values in the citizens of India so that they contribute to the building of an egalitarian society.

8. *Development of Secular Values*: Education must inculcate such values as are helpful in appreciating the diverse religious points of view and harmonising them.

4

Educational Philosophy

SIGNIFICANCE OF PHILOSOPHY

Philosophy is so deeply involved in human life that Aristotle (384-322 BC), the great Greek Philosopher remarked, "Everyone follows a philosophy, whether he is aware of it or not".

Thousands of years ago, Indian seers and thinkers developed a very comprehensive and well-organised system of philosophy for the guidance of the individual.

Francis Bacon (1561-1626), an English philosopher considered philosophy as the 'great' mother of all sciences.

The subject matter of philosophy is as wide as human experience. It is as old as human life. There is no aspect of life, natural or unnatural, animate or inanimate which falls outsides its domain.

Human beings—primitive or civilised, educated or uneducated, plodding or brilliant cannot escape from philosophy. Aldous Huxley (1894-1963) in his book *Ends and Means* has remarked, "Every human being has a philosophy of his own, good or bad, high or low, purely individual or common with others". He has further observed, "Men live in accordance with their philosophy of life, their concern of the world, this is true even of the most thoughtless".

German Philosopher Schopenhauer (1788-1860) remarks "Every man is a born meta-physician". Different fields of philosophy are: economic philosophy, educational philosophy, moral philosophy, physical philosophy, political philosophy and social philosophy.

MEANING AND DEFINITION OF PHILOSOPHY

Sanskrit word *Darshan* (philosophy) means 'direct perception' of the truth. Seers of ancient India used to see or perceive the truth. The same may be said about Socrates (469-399 B.C.), Plato (427-347 B.C.) and Aristotle (384-322 B.C.)—trio of Greek philosophy.

The word 'philosophy' has a Greek origin. '*Philosophia*' a Greek word consists of two words, i.e. '*phileo*' meaning love and '*sophia*' meaning wisdom. Therefore, the literal meaning of philosophy is 'love of wisdom'.

The following definitions of philosophy help us to understand the true meaning of philosophy.

1. *Aristippus* (435-356 B.C.) thinks that philosophy is "the ability to feel at ease in any society".
2. According to *Plato* (472-347 B.C.) "He who has a taste for every sort of knowledge and who is curious to learn and is never satisfied may be justly termed as a philosopher". He has also observed, "Philosophy begins in wonder".
3. According to *Aristotle* (384-322 B.C.), "Philosophy is a science which discovers the real nature of supernatural elements".
4. According to *Cicero, Marcus Tullius* (106-43 B.C.) "Philosophy is the mother of all arts and "the true medicine of mind".
5. *Kant* (1724-1804) regards philosophy as "the science and criticism of cognition".
6. *Kant Immanuel* (1724-1804) regards philosophy as "the science and criticism of cognition".
7. In the words of *Fichte*, (1762-1814), "Philosophy is the science of knowledge".
8. *Coleridge, Samuel Taylor* (1772-1834) defined it as the "Science of Science".
9. *Curtis, George William* (1824-1892) states, "During the course of centuries, the meaning attached to philosophy has undergone many changes, and even in the present

day, thinkers, are not in complete agreement about the aims and subject-matter of this branch of knowledge".

10. *Russell, Bertrand* (1872-1970) states, "Philosophy is to be studied not for the sake of any definite answers to its question... but rather for the sake of the questions themselves, because these questions enlarge our conception of what is possible... but above all because the mind also is rendered great and becomes capable of that union with the universe which constitutes its highest goal".
11. *Radhakrishnan, Sarvapalli* (1888-1975) considers philosophy as "a logical inquiry into the nature of reality".
12. *Huxley, Aldous* (1894-1963) observes, "Men live in accordance with their Philosophy of Life".
13. *Kabir, Humayun* (1902-1969) states that philosophy "seeks to give knowledge of the whole".
14. *Dumery, H.* in his book '*The Problem of God* (1964)' defines philosophy as a "critical reflection on concrete action".
15. *Prof. M. Verma* in book '*The Philosophy of Indian Education* (1969) has explained it as, "(the)... Indian term, *Darshana* as an equivalent to philosophy literally means 'seeing'. The simple physiological act of seeing implies the seen and the 'seer' which is comparatively a good word for the Indian significance of the word philosopher. The 'seeing' is a vision of the entire experienced reality, it is all encompassing, for it is the vision of truth itself". According to Prof. Verma, the term 'philosopher' requires in its derived European sense an intelligent and coherent accounting of the experience of life. It can he arrested at the intellectual level and remain a matter of logical argument. *Darshana* has an extra implication; it includes a 'realisation' an experience of the 'postulated truth' which takes it beyond mere polemics.
16. *Henderson* (1947) thinks that philosophy is a research for "a comprehensive view of nature, an attempt at a universal explanation of the nature of things".
17. In the words of *Bramold*, "Philosophy is a persistent

effort of both ordinary and persistent people to make life as intelligible and meaningful as possible".

18. *R.W. Sellers* has defined philosophy in these words, "Philosophy is a persistent attempt to gain insight into the nature of the world and ourselves by systematic reflection".
19. According to *Brightman*, "Philosophy may be defined as the attempt to think truly about human experience".

Summing Up: From above definitions, it may be concluded that philosophy enquires into the nature of life, reality, truth and values. It tries to understand man and his relationship with the universe. Philosophy is rooted in the search for answers to certain types of problems which a man faces in his life. It provides tentative answers to these problems so that life becomes meaningful and intelligible.

CHIEF CHARACTERISTICS OF PHILOSOPHY

From above definitions we conclude that:

1. Philosophy is a search for reality and truth.
2. Philosophy is based on enquiry.
3. Philosophy is local.
4. Philosophy is a dynamic and living force.
5. Philosophy is an art as well as a science.
6. Philosophy is closely related to education.
7. Philosophy is an intellectual attempt to interpret and understand nature.
8. Philosophy is love of knowledge.
9. Philosophy is love of wisdom.
10. Philosophy is a guide to a way of life.

WHY DO WE NEED PHILOSOPHY?

Philosophy gives a direction to life. Philosophy in India emerged as a result of reflection over the experiences and problems of life. Dr. Radhakrishnan, the great Indian philosopher has suggested this meaning of philosophy through the titles of two of his books. "*The Indian View of Life*" and "*The Idealist View of Life*". Human life is always purposeful. The purpose of life is determined by the philosophy of life.

We need philosophy to take decisions wisely and to act consistently. One needs wisdom to distinguish between two extremes—falsehood and truth, ugliness and beauty, right and wrong etc. Philosophy enables us to live by values for we do not live only by bread, vitamins and technological discoveries.

Social Action and Philosophy

Philosophy furnishes the basis for social action as well as for personal conduct. In the words of *A.C. Ewing* (1964), "Unless we suppose that material wealth is the only thing of value, the inability of philosophy to contribute to this would not mean that it was of no practical value. We value material wealth not for itself... but for its contribution to happiness. Now there is no doubt that one of the most important sources of happiness for those who can enjoy it at all is the search for truth and the contemplation of reality and this is the aim of philosophers".

Philosophers have been instrumental in revolutionary political and social reforms. For example, the American constitution is to a very considerable extent an application of the political ideas of the philosopher John Locke. The ideas of Rousseau played an important role in the French Revolution.

It can be materialistic or spiritualist. In ancient Sparta, the philosophy of life was to defend the country from foreign aggression and thus the aim of life was to become a soldier. The ideal Spartan was an ideal soldier. In Nazi Germany, the philosophy of life was determined by racial superiority and an individual was meant for the state. Similar was the case in communist countries. In ancient India attainment of '*Moksha*' or '*Nirvana*' was the guiding philosophy. In theory at least, 'simple living' and 'high thinking' is the philosophy of life in the present day India.

SCOPE OF PHILOSOPHY: DIFFERENT AREAS OF PHILOSOPHY

Scope of philosophy is so vast that *Cicero* (106-43) B.C., a Roman scholar called it as 'the mother of all arts' and "the true medicine of mind".

Francis Bacon, a great English philosopher regarded the philosophy as, "the great mother of the sciences".

Coleridge (1772-1834) a noted poet considered it as the 'Science of sciences'.

Broadly speaking following types of problems come under the scope of philosophy:

1. Problems of reality
2. Problems of knowledge
3. Problems of value

1. *Problems of Reality*: *'Metaphysics'* is the branch of philosophy which deals with this problem. Questions usually discussed are – What is the nature of the universe we live in? What is reality? Such questions have been raised in the *Upanishads.* Mahatma Buddha called the universe *'Maya'*.

2. *Problems of Knowledge*: This area of philosophy is known as *'Epistemology'*. Questions discussed are: How do we get knowledge? How does a man know what is real? Different philosophers have provided different answers.

3. *Problems of Value*: The branch of philosophy which deals with this problem is 'Axiology'. The problem of values include such questions: What are the principles of life? How do they support the view of reality? Problems of values include standards or norms of conduct.

RELATIONSHIP BETWEEN PHILOSOPHY AND EDUCATION: THEIR INTERDEPENDENCE

Education and philosophy are two sides of the same coin of life. *Sir John Adams* said that education is the dynamic side of philosophy. As *Ross* put it, "Education is the active aspect of philosophical belief, the practical means of realising ideals of life".

T.P. Nunn has said, "Educational aims are correlative to ideals of life".

Henderson has expressed similar views, "Educational aims cannot be determined apart from the ends and aims of life itself for educational aims grow out of life's aims. To determine what constitutes worth living has been one of the chief tasks of philosophy".

Spencer is of the view that "true education is practicable only to true philosophies".

Gentile feels that "Education with philosophy would mean a failure to understand the precise nature of education".

Rusk opines, "From every angle of educational problem comes the demands for a philosophical basis of the subject".

Fichte has rightly observed, "The art of education will never attain complete clearness without philosophy".

Dewey said, "Philosophy is the theory of education in its most general phases. Education is a laboratory in which philosophical directions become concrete and are tested". If education is a set of techniques for imparting knowledge, skills and attitudes philosophy is the foundation to vitalise these. Philosophy is the foundation and education is the super-structure.

Max Black in '*A Note on Philosophy of Education*', Harvard Educational Review (Spring 1956) has very aptly described the relationship in these words, "All serious discussion of educational problems, no matter how specific, soon leads to a consideration of educational aims, and becomes a conversation about the good life, the nature of man, the varieties of experience. But these are the perennial themes of philosophical investigation. It might seem a hard thing to expect educators to be philosophers, but can they be anything else?".

From above it is clear that there is a close interrelationship between philosophy and education. Philosophy points out the way, and education follows it. Education thus becomes the best means for the propagation of philosophy. For the good of life, for the good of the individual and for the good of society, we need direction and this direction is provided exclusively by philosophy, which is the mother of all sciences including education. This, however, does not mean that education is enslaved by philosophy. The field of education provides a testing ground to test the truth of wisdom or direction provided by philosophy. Without the testing ground of education, philosophers would remain arm-chair theorists. A constant mutual interaction goes on between the two. It is therefore said that without philosophy education would be a blind effort and without education, philosophy would be crippled. The chief means of testing the wisdom or follies of philosophy is education which has been described as the 'dynamic side of philosophy'.

It is stated that when we define education as the modification of behaviour the direction in which modification is to be carried out is determined by philosophy. This philosophy deals with the end and education with the means.

ALL GREAT PHILOSOPHERS AS GREAT EDUCATORS

A close analysis of the concept of education as given by various philosophers and educators will make it clear that their views on education are based on their various concepts of reality, of knowledge, of wisdom and of values. The great philosophers of all times have also been great educators. Most of the educational movements were the expressions of their philosophical beliefs. Views of great thinkers like Socrates, Plato, Aristotle, Comenius, John Locke, Rousseau, Froebel, Dewey, H.G. Wells, Bertrand Russell, A.N. Whitehead and Aldous Huxley, offer an interesting example of the intimate connection between philosophy and education. The ancient sages in India were all educational philosophers. In recent times, this is fully illustrated in the case of Swami Dayananda, Swami Vivekananda, Sri Aurobindo, Gurudev Tagore, Dr. Radhakrishnan, Gandhiji, etc.

DEPENDENCE OF PHILOSOPHY ON EDUCATION

There is no doubt that almost all philosophers promote their philosophy through education. Following are the reasons on account of which it is said that philosophy depends on education:

1. *Education Serves as the Base*: This implies that an educated person alone is capable of thinking coherently, methodology and systematically.
2. *Education as Transmitter as Promoter of Philosophy*: Education keeps philosophy alive by transmitting philosophy from one generation to another. Teachers through their examples, textbooks and other media promote philosophy.
3. *Education as the Tester of Philosophy*: Education is the testing ground of philosophical ideas and theory. It serves as the laboratory for theory (philosophy).
4. *Education Provides Form and Shape to Philosophical Ideas*: Adams has very rightly observed, "Education is the dynamic side of philosophy. Philosophy is the contemplative side of a theory or problems while education is the active side".
5. *Education as the Translator of Philosophical Principles into Practice*: Philosophy determines the aims of life and education translates these into practice.

DEPENDENCE OF EDUCATION ON PHILOSOPHY

Following are the views of scholars which demonstrate that education depends upon philosophy:

1. *Dewey*: "Philosophy is the theory of education in its most general phase."
2. *Fichte*: "The art of education will never attain complete clearness without philosophy."
3. *Gentile*: "Education without philosophy would mean a failure to understand the precise nature of education."

4. *Ross*: "All educational questions are ultimately the questions of philosophy."
5. *Rusk*: "Philosophy formulates what it conceives to be the end of life, education offers suggestions how this end is to be achieved."
6. *Spencer*: "True education is practicable only by a true philosophy."

SIGNIFICANCE OF STUDYING PHILOSOPHY IN UNDERSTANDING EDUCATIONAL PRACTICES AND TRENDS: CONTRIBUTION OF PHILOSOPHY TO EDUCATION

A study of philosophy is very helpful in understanding the following practices and trends in education. In other words we can say that following is the contribution of philosophy to education.

1. Philosophy and Educational Aims
2. Philosophy and Curriculum
3. Philosophy and Textbooks
4. Philosophy and Methods of Teaching
5. Philosophy and Discipline
6. Philosophy and the Teacher
7. Philosophy and Educational Organisation, Administration and Supervision

1. *Philosophy and Aims in Education*: "No system of education", says *Acharya J.B. Kripalani*, the noted Gandhian philosopher, "can be properly appraised and appreciated, unless it is studied in connection with the ideas and ideals which it represents". The Soviet System of education of the old could properly be understood only in the light of the philosophy of Marxism and Leninism. To gain insight into the British system of education, it is necessary to have the correct perspective of the synthesis between the progressivism and the conservation which the Butler Act tried to achieve.

In Ancient Sparta, the ideal was to defend the country's

honour and hence the aim of the Spartan System of education was to prepare citizens to be soldiers and patriots. On the other hand, the Athenian system of education aimed at the cultural development of each individual, in conformity with the Athenian philosophy of that era.

During the British Period, the rulers were guided by their philosophy of imperialism and accordingly formulated the system of education in India.

The aims of education in independent India have been determined by the philosophy underlying our Constitution.

The aim of education has a reference to the ideals or philosophy of a nation. In independent India, philosophy of life is enshrined in the Preamble of its Constitution. Educational aims accordingly draw their inspiration from it. The aims of education in the USA are based on its democratic philosophy. The philosophy of fascism determined the aims of education in Germany during Hitler's time. The philosophy of communism influenced the aims of education in Russia and China.

2. *Philosophy and Curriculum*: The philosophical approach to life is the guiding factor in the determination of the curriculum. Gandhiji's scheme of basic education was an expression of his philosophy. He was against the lopsidedness of the system of education as propounded by Lord Macaulay and was moved by the illiteracy and poverty of the people. His scheme of studies, therefore, emphasised crafts and the environment. He was very keen to make education self-supporting besides developing moral character. The National Policy on Education 1986 lays stress on a Core Curriculum keeping in view the needs of emotional and national integration.

Introduction of self-government in school programme is the outcome of democratic philosophy.

Various philosophies like humanism, idealism, pragmatism and naturalism have influenced curriculum in varying degrees.

Following examples illustrate the influence of philosophy on curriculum formulation:

(a) Individuals, nations and societies have philosophies of life. The aim of life in Ancient Sparta was to live as a soldier. The philosophy of life stressed the development of physical skills and well-trained persons. The philosophy of life was to become an ideal soldier. Content of education, therefore, emphasised physical training and strength.

(b) The Nazi Germany or the Hitler regime believed that the German people were superior to all other races. The system of education in Nazi Germany aimed at producing those Germans who considered themselves superior to all other human beings. Curriculum, text-books, methods of teaching, etc. were geared to this philosophy.

(c) The philosophy of life in a democratic society emphasises the development of individuality. Educational theory and methodology include all processes which enable the individual to develop democratic ideals.

(d) The philosophy of life in our country in ancient times was based upon spiritualism. People believed in simple living and high thinking. The system of education strove hard for attaining salvation by leading a pure and simple life. Accordingly, the scheme of studies was determined.

(e) The Indian sages and seers converted their forest homes into educational institutions in accordance with their philosophy of life. The philosophy of life of Lord Buddha was practised and preached through a well-organised system of monasteries which were also great centres of Buddhist education. Curriculum was formulated accordingly.

(f) Contents of education during the British period were determined by their philosophy which emphasised that Indians should be educated in such a way so as to make them Indian in blood and colour but English in dress, manners and tastes. Also, they wanted to prepare clerks to assist the Britishers to carry out their administration. Thirdly, they were interested in the export of raw materials from India for their manufacturing industries in England. Thus they neglected teaching of Indian culture, philosophy and religion. They also neglected vocational education in the curriculum.

(g) Education in independent India is expected to train the children in accordance with the philosophy as enshrined in our Constitution. Thus the contents of education include material on developing the values of secularism, socialism and democracy.

(h) Recently, far reaching changes have taken place in the erstwhile USSR which now comprises a number of Independent States. The philosophy of communism has received a set back and democratic values have gained prominence. Accordingly democratic ideals are also taken note of in the educational system of the Russian Federation.

3. *Philosophy and Textbooks*: The contents of the textbooks must mirror the philosophy or way of life of the people. In a socialist society textbooks emphasise socialist philosophy. In a state dominated and ruled by religious leaders, textbooks reflect tenets of scriptures. In India, since independence, there has been a great stress on emotional integration and national unity. Accordingly textbooks are being screened from time to time to ensure that they include that matter also which promoters emotional integration and national unity.

4. *Philosophy and Methods of Teaching*: Every school of philosophy has its own methods of teaching. According to the philosophy of idealism, question-answer method, lecture method and discussion method are most suitable methods of education. Naturalism recommends learning by doing, learning by self-experience and direct experience. Pragmatic philosophy advocates project method, problem solving method and socialist techniques. It is through methods that the teacher

establishes contact between the child and subject-matter. Rousseau, Fichte and Froebel assume that the child's nature is good and needs perfect freedom in its working. Any intervention with it is wrong. All modern methods are paedo-centric at least in theory. The importance of the educand is stressed in the process of education more than the subject-matter or educator. Under the influence of these philosophic views, the new education holds that the teacher should prepare the environment as best as he can and then leave children alone. Neill's Summer School and the Project Method are the results of these philosophies.

5. *Philosophy and Discipline*: Discipline also, like the curriculum, textbooks and methods of teaching, reflects the philosophy of life accepted at a particular time more directly than any other aspect of school work. In other words, philosophy of an age is reflected in the discipline of its educational institutions. Discipline even reflects the political philosophy prevalent in the country. In a despotic system of government, repression is common. In a democracy, the doctrine of emancipation is advocated as a disciplinary measure.

In a democratic set up, discipline is viewed as inner discipline as well as social discipline based on group work. In the totalitarian state, discipline is regimented and assumes the form of a military discipline, and is based on fear of the teacher and the head. There is little concern for the individuality of the child in a totalitarian type of discipline. The idealists emphasise the impact of impression of the teacher on his students. 'Free discipline' is the slogan of the naturalist.

6. *Philosophy and the Teacher*: A teacher is said to play an important role in shaping and moulding the ideals, habits, manners, tastes and ways of life and above all the character and personality of the students. It is, therefore, very essential that he must have a consistent and sound philosophy in accordance with the philosophy of the nation to which he belongs.

7. *Philosophy and Educational Organisation, Administration and Supervision*: Democratic philosophy lays emphasis on the participation of the staff and the students in running some

programmes of the educational institutions. Philosophy of communism provides little scope for such involvement and the head decides everything.

Conclusion: Thus we find that the formation of aims, the choice of a suitable curriculum or even textbooks, the use of proper methods and devices, the decision about the type of discipline to be maintained and how to maintain it, the creation of general tone in the school are ultimately questions of philosophy and a knowledge of all these is very essential to make education purposeful, inspirational and effective.

Idealism has given us an all-inclusive view of education. It has led to the promotion of self-realisation as an aim of education. Naturalism has paved the way for the psychological and scientific trends in education. Realism emphasises the content value and gives an important place to diversified curricula. Pragmatism stresses the practical and social aspects. Humanism extols human values and thoughts and respects human personality. Existentialism stresses the values of free thinking.

SIGNIFICANCE OF PHILOSOPHY TO THE TEACHER

Education is a practical activity. Every educational practice is illuminated with the backdrop of philosophy. The speculative, normative and critical function of philosophy affects not only the direction of moral guidance that the teacher gives but also affects the direction and the emphasis on the curriculum, the teacher's attitudes from day to day, even from hour to hour. No practice is good and scientific unless rooted in philosophical thought which gives logic, rationale, sequence and system to education. Since philosophy speaks the language of analysis and reason, there is hardly any problem of the teacher which is not solved by philosophy.

A basic understanding of philosophical themes on the part of all teachers regarding ancient and contemporary philosophical systems of thought will enable them to reorient their own philosophy and beliefs, help them to understand the problematic situations in the classroom discipline, under-achievement of students and many such other problems, and ultimately enable them to determine the manner in which they will handle these problems.

The naturalists insist that the teacher should never interfere with the free activities of children. He is simply to set the educational environment. The idealists advocate that the teacher's role should be that of the head of a family. Pupils should be inspired by his personality and develop full faith in him. According to pragmatists, the teacher is not to impose anything on the pupils. He is simply to provide opportunity to his pupils for activity and learning. However, a teacher should not be wedded to any of these philosophies. He should derive inspiration from all the philosophies and try to imbibe the best features of every philosophy.

For a teacher working in Indian schools, the philosophic values enshrined in the Constitution should be the guidelines.

Philosophy helps the teacher in the following manner:

1. Philosophy provides direction to the teacher.
2. Philosophy serves as a guide to the teacher for experiments.
3. Philosophy provides clarification of the nature of education to the teacher.
4. Philosophy enables the teacher to think critically, constructively and rationally.
5. Philosophy enables the teacher to handle disciplinary situations satisfactorily.

The following points should help the teacher to understand the relationship between education and philosophy.

1. *Why to Educate*? This is concerned with the aims of education as determined by philosophy. The teacher and the taught must be very clear about the aims of education so that right efforts are made in the right direction. In fact this is the most important aspect of education which is based on philosophies. All other aspects of education i.e. the curriculum,

the methods of teaching and the type of discipline etc. are dependent on the aims. The entire educational system is subservient to the fulfilment of these aims. In this sense, it is sometimes stated that the most important contribution of philosophy to education is in the domain of determining aims of education.

2. *Whom to Educate*? The teacher must understand that child is a living being and he is to be enabled to understand the philosophical values enshrined in the Constitution.

3. *What are the Contents of Education*? This leads to the contents of the curriculum. The contents are to be taught in accordance with philosophical thought.

4. *Who is to Educate*? The teacher is to educate and he must understand himself in the context of the philosophy of the society in which he lives.

5. *Where to Educate*? The teacher must understand that school is a place where the principles of philosophy are put into use. Besides, school is not the only agency for this purpose. There are other agencies also to translate philosophical thought into practice. The teacher should keep this aspect in view.

6. *How to Educate*? This involves the techniques of imparting information and knowledge so that children acquire wisdom to make their lives worth living. This also relates to type of discipline needed.

Summing up: As observed by *Gentile,* "The belief that men may continue to educate without concerning themselves with philosophy means a failure to understand the precise nature of education. The process of education cannot go on the right lines without the help of philosophy. Since philosophy speaks the language of analysis and reason, there is hardly any problem of education which is difficult to solve by the teacher who possesses the clear lights of philosophy".

5

Major Philosophies and their Impact on Education

IDEALISM IN EDUCATION

IDEALISM AS THE OLDEST PHILOSOPHY

Idealism is usually considered as the oldest philosophy. It is on account of the philosophy of idealism that humanity can be saved from the destructive wars and dazzling materialism. Idealism in India is as old as the *Vedas*. The Vedic seers were great idealists. The *Upanishads* and the *Bhagwad Gita* made a very comprehensive analysis of idealism. In the West, Plato—a Greek philosopher (427-347 BC) was a great idealist.

The following views of great thinkers point out the meaning and dimensions of idealism:

1. According to *Kath Upanishad*, an idealist is one who possesses supreme knowledge by concentration of mind.
2. In the words of *Rusk*, "Idealism contends that the material and physical universe known to science is an incomplete expression of reality, that it exists but to subserve, and requires to compliment it a higher type of reality, a spiritual universe." Rusk regards human personality as the 'noblest work of God'.
3. According to *Ross*, "Idealistic philosophy takes many and varied forms, but to postulate underlying all is that mind or spirit in the essential world-stuff, that the true reality is of a mental character."

4. *Horne* defines idealism in these words, "Educational philosophy of idealism is an account of man finding himself as an integral part of a universe of mind."
5. *Brubacher* explains idealism in these words, "Idealists point out that it is mind that is central in understanding the world. To them nothing gives a greater sense of reality than the activity of the mind engaged in trying to comprehend the world."
6. *Harold Titus*. "Idealism asserts that reality consists of ideas, materialism thoughts, minds or and selves rather than materials, objects and force."

Summing up: Idealism contends that spiritual aspects are the chief aspects of human life. Natural or scientific facets of life are subordinate to spiritual ones. When the emphasis is on the spiritual aspect, it is called idealism or philosophy of idealism. The idealist 'idolise' the mind beyond everything. Idealism exalts human personality.

Chief Exponents of Idealism

Eastern Idealists: (i) Vedic seers, (ii) The Upanishads and Gita, (iii) Swami Dayananda, (iv) Swami Vivekananda, (v) Mahatma Gandhi, (vi) Rabindranath Tagore, (vii) Sri Aurobindo.

Western Idealists: (i) Plato—a Greek philosopher (427-347 B.C.), (ii) Kant—a German philosopher (1724-1804 A.D.), (iii) Froebel—a German philosopher (1772-1852 A.D.), (iv) William T. Haris—an American philosopher (1835-1909 A.D.).

FUNDAMENTAL PRINCIPLES OF IDEALISM

The essence of idealism is contained in the Upanishads. The '*Britharanayaka Upanishad*' states.

Asato ma sad gamaya,
Tamaso me jyotir gamaya,
Mrtyor ma amartam gamaya,
(Lead me from unreal to the real,

Lead me from darkness to light,
Lead me from death to immortality)
According to '*Katha Upanishad*'
Yastu vijnanauan bhauati
Tasyendriyani vasyani
Sadasvaiya saratheh
(He who is possessed of supreme knowledge by concentration of mind must have his senses under control, like spirited steeds controlled by a charioteer)

In brief, following are the main principles of idealism:

1. God is the source of all creation.
2. God is the source of all knowledge.
3. Spirit and mind constitute reality.
4. Material and physical universe is not a complete expression of reality.
5. Material and physical universe is subordinate to a higher type of reality—a spiritual universe, a universe of ideas and values.
6. Spiritual world is more important than the material.
7. Values are eternal, absolute and unchanging.
8. What is ultimately real is not the object itself but the ideal or idea behind it.
9. Man being spiritual is a supreme creation.
10. Man is not the creation of his environment in the sense the term is applied to animals.
11. Man needs some encouragement or light in the face of darkness.
12. There are intrinsic moral and spiritual values.
13. Reality is to be found in man's mind rather than in material nature.
14. Study of man's nature and his mind is more important than the study of material universe.
15. Man has a spiritual nature which expresses itself in the form of intellectual culture, morality and religion.

IDEALISM ON VARIOUS DIMENSIONS OF EDUCATION

1. *Aims of Education according to Idealism*: The most important contribution of idealism to the field of education is that it has provided human life with high aims. It has set out aims of education very clearly. In a world threatened by materialism where technology has taken away much of man's freedom and dignity, the idealist philosophy restores man to his proper place in the universe. The idealists very rightly point out that the aim of education is not merely to enable the individual to produce more material goods but to exalt human personality. Sri Aurobindo, in this regard has observed, "The acquiring of various kinds of information is only one and not the chief aim of education, its central aim is the building of the powers of the human mind and spirit, it is the formation or, as I would prefer to view it, the evoking of knowledge, character and culture—that at least if no more. And the distinction makes an enormous difference." Tagore also believes, "The object of education is the freedom of mind which can only be achieved through the path of freedom" *R.W. Everson* has expressed this very view in the following verses:

Not gold, but only men can make

A people great and strong

The University Education Commission (1948-49) headed by Dr. S. Radhakrishnan has very beautifully stated the aim of education from the view of an idealist, "If we wish to bring about a savage upheaval in our society, a '*Rakshas raj*', all that we need to do is to give vocational and technical education and starve the spirit. We will have a number of scientists without conscience, technicians without taste who find a void within themselves, a moral vacuum."

According to *Froebel*, "The object of education is the realisation of a faithful, pure, inviolable and hence holy life."

In the words of *J.S. Ross*, "The aim of education specially associated with idealism is the exhalation of personality or self-realisation."

According to *Rusk*, "Education must enable mankind through its culture to enter more and more fully into spiritual realm, and also enlarge the boundaries of spiritual realm."

Aims of education according to idealism may be summed up as under:

(i) Exhalation of human personality—unfolding the divine in man.
(ii) Self-realisation by man.
(iii) Development of will power.
(iv) Development of character.
(v) Development of rational attitude.
(vi) Transmission of spiritual and cultural heritage.
(vii) Universal education for universal individual.
(viii) Development of moral values which falls into two categories:
  (a) Duties to self which include physical fitness, self-culture, industriousness, etc.
  (b) Duties to others i.e. respect for and appreciation of the opinion of others, cooperativeness, generosity, liberality, etc.
(ix) Preparation for a holy life.
(x) To cultivate the values of truth, beauty and goodness.

While discussing aims of education, it must be kept in view that idealism does not ignore the vocational aim of education. It simply gives it secondary importance.

2. *Curriculum and Idealism.* Idealism stresses three values of 'truth', 'goodness' and 'beauty'. These three values determine three types of human activities—intellectual, moral and aesthetic. Each type of activity is represented by studies or subjects that should form a part of the curriculum. The following arrangement of the curriculum is recommended by idealism.

Value	*Subject/Activity*
1. Truth	1. It is represented by intellectual subjects or activities. This includes subjects like humanities, languages, social sciences and physical sciences.
2. Goodness	2. This includes subjects like ethics, metaphysics and religion, etc.
3. Beauty	3. Aesthetic subjects or activities like art and poetry etc. relate to this part of the curriculum.

Ross's scheme for a complete curriculum in the light of idealism is as under:

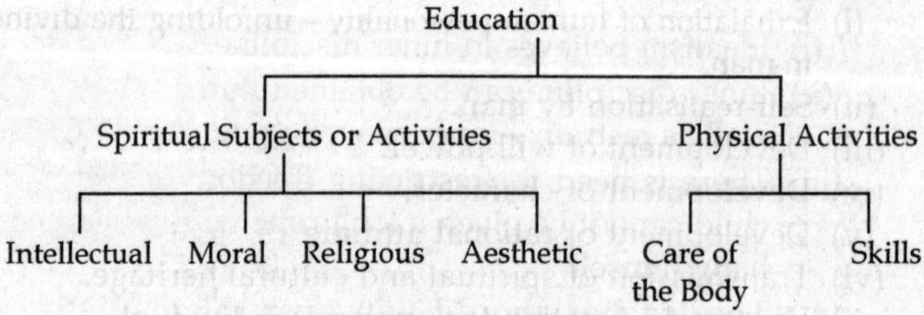

Fig. 5.1: Curriculum

Chief features of curriculum in idealism are:

(i) Curriculum should include those subjects and activities which emphasise higher values of life.
(ii) Curriculum should provide a place of prominence to humanities.
(iii) Ethics and religion should find an important place in the curriculum.

3. *Idealism and Methods of Teaching*: The idealist suggests the following techniques and methods of teaching:

(i) Narration
(ii) Explanation
(iii) Exposition
(iv) Questioning
(v) Discussion
(vi) Practice and Repetition
(vii) Conversational Method
(viii) Inductive and Deductive
(ix) Contemplation and Reflection

4. *Idealism and Discipline*: While 'freedom' is the slogan of the naturalists, 'discipline' is that of idealists. Disciplining the mind and body of the child are the watchwords of the idealists. An idealist attaches great importance to the guidance of the

teacher to the child for realising his 'self'. Suggested features of discipline according to idealists are:

(i) Idealism believes in inner discipline.
(ii) Inner discipline can be obtained through guidance as well as restrain—inner as well as outer or external.
(iii) There is need for restricting freedom of the child. A child cannot be given a long rope with which he may hang himself.
(iv) The teacher should win over the child through 'impression', i.e., good personal examples of behaviour and conduct. The child especially in the plastic period of his early life considers the teacher to be an ideal person to be emulated by the pupils.
(v) Participation in social service activities develops spirit of sacrifice—an important feature of the life of an ideal person.

5. *Idealism and the Teacher*: Teacher assumes an important place in idealism. He is the key figure in the educative process. His personality is the most vital influence on the education of the child. A child is greatly influenced by his conduct, his way of speech, his etiquette etc.

Idealism considers the teacher a friend, philosopher and guide to his pupils. He guides them in such a way as they may attain 'self-realisation'. Character development and value development are the most important concerns of the teacher.

Froebel's metaphor of the Kindergarten, perhaps, explains best the functions of the educator. The school is regarded as a garden and teacher as the gardener whose function is to tend the little human plants in his charge carefully and to help them to grow to beauty and perfection. The human plant can grow unaided according to the laws of its own nature, yet the gardener is to see that plant attains its finest form; it produces or gives the finest results. Ross has beautifully summed up the place of the teacher in the idealistic school when he says, "The naturalist may be content with briars but the idealist wants fine roses. So the educator by his efforts must assist the educand who is developing according to the laws of his nature, to attain levels that would otherwise be denied to him."

In the words of *Gentile*, "Teacher is a spiritual symbol of right conduct."

According to *Swami Vivekananda*, "What you call the personal magnetism of man—that is what goes out and impresses you."

In the words of *Sri Aurobindo*, "If you wish to be respected by your child, have respect for yourself and be at every moment worthy of respect".

Lauri has said, "If a teacher has not an ideal aim he had better take to shopkeeping".

According to idealism, main functions of a teacher are:

(i) The teacher must assume the role of a Guru.
(ii) The teacher must understand his pupils thoroughly.
(iii) The teacher must be a personal friend and guide to his pupils.
(iv) The teacher should present high standards of behaviour and conduct before his pupils.
(v) The teacher should have a deep knowledge of his subject.
(vi) The teacher should strive hard for providing such a social environment in the classroom that is conducive to imitation by students.
(vii) The teacher should aim at inculcating in the pupils a desire to work hard.
(viii) The teacher should employ thought provoking techniques and thereby encourage his pupils to think for themselves. Just as one cannot teach a subject without a knowledge of it, similarly it is not possible to impart knowledge to a pupil without knowing him. The teacher aims at inculcating in the pupils a desire to work hard by assigning definite tasks to each of the students—the tasks being suited to individual capacity. Questioning and discussion are the main techniques

employed by a teacher in the classroom. Classroom environment should encourage constructive thinking.

LIMITATIONS AND WEAKNESSES OF IDEALISM

1. *Subtle Concepts*: Concepts like 'spirit', 'mind', 'soul', 'the cosmos', etc. inherent in idealism have little relevance in classroom teaching.
2. *Nothing Like Spiritual Universe*: The spiritualist theory of spiritual universe as stated by idealists is not considered to be in consonance with the scientific research today.
3. *Over Emphasis on Models*: The idealism in education stresses limitation of models but younger generation prefers invention and originally rather than imitation.
4. *Over Emphasis on Good Manners*: Idealists' too much emphasis on good manners, and modesty may be mistaken for diffidence.
5. *Undue Stress on Information*: Idealism's emphasis on gaining knowledge is likely to turn educational institutions as information-mongers' workshops. School curricula becomes overloaded with obsolete knowledge sometimes.
6. *Ignoring Overall Development of Personality*: Scheme of education based on idealism, by and large, pays less attention to physical, industrial, social and electronic environment of today.
7. *Obsolete Theories*: Obsolete knowledge may create hindrance in infusing new spirit in the contents.
8. *Ignoring ITC*: In general, it is stated that the idealist view in education pays less attention to the present environment dominated by Information Communication Technology (ICT).
9. *Rigorous and Strict Concept of Discipline*: The idealists lay too much emphasis on 'Does' and 'Don'ts'.
10. *Rather Unpsychological*: Idealism parts more emphasis on philosophical concepts and neglects psychological aspects.

11. *Under-rating Science and Technology*: Idealism does not give due place to the development in science and technology.
12. *Less Emphasis on Social Side*: Idealism does not assign proper place to the social aspect of the personality.

CONTRIBUTION OF IDEALISM TO EDUCATIONAL THEORY AND PRACTICE

1. *Right Emphasis on Higher Values*: The present world seems to be plagued with materialism which ignores higher values of life. Idealism aims restoring man to his proper place.
2. *Recognition of Rich Heritage*: Idealism holds that the past culture must be given its due place in any scheme of educational reconstruction.
3. *Due Regard to Human Personality*: The present machine and electronic age treats the human being as a machine. Idealism warns against this type of approach.
4. *Important Place to the Teacher*: Idealism assigns an important place to the teacher in the educative process.
5. *Realisation of Self*: Idealism insists that for the realisation of the 'self', every human being must receive an opportunity to be educated. Thus the goal of the idealist in this context is universal education.
6. *Human Relations*: Emphasis of the idealist on personality development has provided a fresh look at human relations in teaching.
7. *Aims of Education*: Idealism provides clear guidelines for determining aims in education, curricular, discipline, teacher's role and methods of teaching-learning.
8. *Self-Discipline*: Idealism rightly regards self-discipline as the only way for the development of the child.

Summing Up: In a world threatened by materialism, the philosophy of idealism provides light and direction to man for restoring his proper place. The need of the hour is to develop higher values among students. This lead must come from leaders—political, religious and all those who occupy high places in different walks of life. They must set good examples. Educational institutions alone cannot develop higher values of life. Of course, they must take all possible steps to develop higher values in students.

PHILOSOPHY OF NATURALISM IN EDUCATION

Meaning of Naturalism

With a view to have a clear perspective, we may take up a few definitions given by eminent philosophers:

1. In the words of *Hocking*, "Naturalism is metaphysics which considers nature as the whole of reality. It excludes what is supernatural or the other world."
2. *James Ward's* view is, "Naturalism is the doctrine which separates nature from God, subordinates spirit to matter and sets up unchangeable laws as supreme."
3. According to *Rusk*, "Naturalism is a philosophical position adopted by those who approach philosophy from purely scientific point of view."
4. *Perry* defines naturalism as, "Naturalism is not science but an assertion about science. More especially, it is the assertion that scientific knowledge is final leaving no room for extra-scientific or philosophical knowledge."
5. *Adams* views naturalism as "Naturalism is a term loosely applied in educational theory to systems of training that are not dependent on school and books but on the actual life of the educand."
6. In the words of *Joyce*, "Naturalism is a system whose salient characteristic is the exclusion of whatever is spiritual or indeed whatever is transcendental of experience from our philosophy of nature and man."
7. *Thomas and Lang* define Naturalism as "Naturalism holds that ultimate reality is material world not spiritual world".

Summing up: 'Return to nature', and break the chains of society' are the watchwords of the naturalists. There is nothing beyond nature.

CHIEF CHARACTERISTICS OF NATURALISM

These are as under:

1. *Supremacy of Nature*: Man is subordinate to nature. There is nothing like 'Supernaturalism'. All values exist in nature.
2. *Belief in Nature*: The naturalists think that everything is nature. Nature alone is the source of all knowledge.
3. *Belief in Science*: According to naturalists, scientific knowledge is final. Science reveals the mysteries of nature.
4. *Materialism is a Reality*: The real world is the material world.
5. *No Faith in Soul*: Naturalism has no faith in soul or spirit. It does not believe in divinity. Human life is interpreted in terms of matter only.
6. *Goodness of the Nature of Man*: A naturalist thinks that everything that comes to us from nature is good but it degenerates in the hands of man.
7. *Equality*: Naturalists regard that in the natural order of things all human beings are equal.
8. *Senses as the Gateways of Knowledge*: Naturalists are very emphatic that all knowledge comes through the senses. The senses are eye, ear, nose, tongue and skin. Knowledge gathered through these is more lasting.
9. *Relative Nature of Values*: Values are created in terms of specific needs.
10. *Creation of Societies*: Man creates societies to meet some of its needs.
11. *Several Illusions*: Moral instinct, innate conscience, providence, power of prayer and freedom of will, etc. are all illusions.
12. *Denial of Supernaturalism*: Naturalism gives little significance to concepts like God, spirit or divine.

Types of Naturalism

(1) Biological Naturalism

(2) Mechanical Naturalism

(3) Physical Sciences Naturalism

Prominent Naturalist Philosophers

1. Bacon, Francis (1561-1626 A.D.), English philosopher
2. Comenius, John (1529-1670 A.D.), Czechslovakian philosopher
3. Rousseau, Jean Jacques (1712-1877), French (Swiss born) philosopher
4. Spencer, Herbert (1820-1903 A.D.), English philosopher
5. Tagore, Rabindranath (1861-1941), Indian philosopher

NATURALISM AND ITS VARIOUS DIMENSIONS OF EDUCATION (IMPLICATIONS OF NATURALISM IN EDUCATION)

1. Principles of Education according to Naturalism

1. Naturalism accords an important place to the child in the educative process.
2. Naturalism advocates education in accordance with the nature of the child.
3. Naturalism considers natural environment as an important source of education.
4. Naturalism gives an important place to the present life of the child and makes it the basis of education.
5. Naturalism states that adequate freedom should be given to the child in the educative process.
6. Naturalism has an insignificant place for acquiring knowledge from books.

2. Naturalism and Educational Aims

1. *Redirection of the Impulses of the Child*: Education should aim at sublimating, redirecting and coordinating the natural impulses of the child for the attainment of

natural goals, i.e., the common good of the individual and the society.

2. *Preparing for Struggle for Existence*: The aim of education, should be to equip the individual for the struggle for existence and thus ensure his survival.
3. *Living in Harmony with Nature*: Education should enable an individual to live in harmony with his surroundings and environments by teaching him how to adopt and adjust to those environments.
4. *Conformity with Nature*: Rousseau's aim of education is the development of the child in conformity with nature.
5. *Training for Complete Life*: According to *Herbert Spencer*, education should be a preparation and training for a complete life.
6. *Development According to Natural Ability*: *Rousseau J. Jacques* says that the aim of education should be to develop the child according to his ability.
7. *Development of Individuality*: *T.N. Nunn* thinks that the aim should be to enable the child to develop his individuality and contribute to society.
8. *Struggling Successfully*: *Darwin* states that the aim of education should be to enable the child struggle successfully for his survival.

3. Study of the Child and Child-Centred Education

Naturalism considers a child as the 'Hero' in the drama of education. Naturalists lay emphasis on the nature of the child, his study and the various stages of development through which he passes. The child is born as innocent, simple and pure at heart. His nature is essentially good. Rousseau asserts that the child is not an adult; he is not to be judged from the standards of an adult. Education should be in accordance with the nature of each stage.

4. Naturalism and Curriculum

Although there are divergent views of the naturalists on curriculum contents, they agree on the following points:

1. *Education according to 3 A's*: Curriculum should cater to the age, ability and aptitudes, of the child.
2. *Need Based Curriculum*: Curriculum should be constructed to meet the needs of the child according to the nature of development at each stage.
3. *Emphasis on Self-Preserving Subjects*: It lays stress on the subjects which are helpful in the self-preservation of man.
4. *Basic Sciences*: Naturalism stress basic sciences.
5. *Physical and Health Sciences*: It gives importance to physical and health sciences.

5. The Teacher

Merely an Observer: According to the naturalists, the teacher is not to play the role of a 'giver' of information, ideas and ideals, of a 'moulder' of will-power and character. He is not to interfere with the activities of children. He must not impose himself on them. His duty is to see that their education is the free development of their interests and motives rather than an artificial effort made by him. He should only be an observer of child's development from outside the scene. In fact a teacher should be an 'Observer', 'Protector' and 'Stage setter'.

6. Naturalism and Methods of Teaching

1. *Experience is the Best Teacher*: *Rousseau* advises, "Give your scholar no verbal lessons; he should be taught by experience".
2. *Observation Method*: The child should observe things and discover for himself.
3. *Individualised Instruction*: According to a naturalist, every child has the ability to acquire knowledge and to benefit the individual. Hence the method of class teaching is not useful.
4. *Self-Education*: The naturalist advocates that the child is expected to acquire information, knowledge and, ideas by himself.

5. *Things rather than Words*: *Rousseau* says, "Teach by doing whatever you can, and only fall back upon words when doing is out of question".
6. *Social Learning through Participation*: A child acquires social learning when he takes part in the social activities.

7. Naturalism and Discipline

1. *Discipline by Natural Consequences*: The concept of discipline according to idealists may be expressed in four words, "Discipline by natural consequences". Natural consequences are those experiences which the child receives by following an activity. When the child runs its head against the table, he feels pain. The remembrance of pain makes the child disciplined.
2. *No Punishments*: *Rousseau* states, "Children should never receive punishment as such, it should always come as the natural consequences of his action". If a child is late for a picnic party, let him learn from this experience of being late.
3. *Full Freedom to the Child*: A naturalist starts with the assumption that the nature of child is essentially good. Therefore, he should be given freedom of expression and development.
4. *School Organisation as a Free Society*: According to the naturalists, the school should provide an environment which is conducive to the free development of the growing child. The whole school should be organised into a free, natural society where each child contributes to her or his well-being and where the pupils learn how to lead and how to follow. A system of self-government should, in short, be introduced.

8. Negative Education

Rousseau's curriculum for Emile is based on the principle of negative education. Negative education, according to him, is one that:

(i) tends to perfect the organs that are the instruments of knowledge, before giving this knowledge directly, and

(ii) endeavours to prepare the way for reason by the proper exercise of the senses.

The doctrine of negative education as applied to physical education demands the greatest possible freedom for child in his movement and exercises, simple diet, loose or scanty and light clothing etc. When applied to intellectual education it would amount to absence of verbal lessons, books or any positive studies.

LIMITATIONS OF NATURALISM IN EDUCATION

1. *No Clear Cut Goals*: Naturalism does not offer definite aims of education.
2. *Neglect of Books*: There is a very minor place for books. We cannot neglect the treasure of knowledge contained in the pointed materials.
3. *Negligible Importance to Higher Values*: Naturalism by and large, ignores the higher ends in the process of education.
4. *Undue Emphasis on Education through Nature*: It is certain that physical nature alone cannot be considered adequate for providing all education.
5. *Absolute Freedom a Myth*: Absolute freedom does not exist. It never existed. It will never exist in a civilised society. "Child cannot be given the long rope to hang himself."
6. *Very Little Role for the Teacher*: Naturalism minimises the role of the teacher in the educative process. Even in the electronic age, a teacher occupies an important place in the teaching-learning process.
7. *Neglect of Moral and Spiritual Values*: Naturalism ignores the moral and spiritual development of the child.

CONTRIBUTION OF NATURALISM TO EDUCATION

1. *Child Centred/Learner Centred Education*: Naturalism has brought to the forefront the importance of the recognition of child in the process of education.

2. *Significance of the Study of the Child*: Naturalism has very clearly drawn the attention of the educators to study child carefully and provide education accordingly. It advocates that education, should be 'child centred'.
3. *Enjoyable Process of Education*: Naturalism has stressed that the educative process should be made pleasurable and enjoyable.
4. *Educational Institutions in Natural Surroundings*: Naturalism indicates that educational institutions should be set up in natural surroundings.
5. *Stress or Progressive Methods of Teaching*: Naturalism brings to light the significance, of progressive methods of teaching like 'learning by doing', 'learning by observing' and 'learning by inductive approach'.
6. *New Movements in Education*: Naturalism has given birth to new movements and new types of educational institutions like A.S. Neill's Summer School and Visvabharati.

Summing up: The most important contribution of naturalism is that it has given birth to progressive methods of instruction in accordance with the nature of the child. It is usually said that naturalism has psycholigised education.

PRAGMATISM

Derivative Meaning of Pragmatism

Pragmatism is also known by various names such as 'Practical Philosophy', 'Worldly-wise Philosophy', Utilitarian Philosophy, 'Down to Earth Philosophy' 'Experimental Philosophy', 'Philosophy of Instrumentalism', 'Philosophy of Consequentialism', 'Practical Philosopy' and 'Cash Philosophy' on account of its emphasis on 'utility' aspect.

The word 'pragmatism' is derived from a Greek word '*Pragma*' which means 'to do', 'to make', and 'to accomplish'. Therefore words 'doing', 'making', 'accomplishing' etc. are used while referring to pragmatism. Expressions like 'action', 'practice' and 'activity' have become popular in education on account of pragmatism.

Pragmatism stands between idealism and naturalism.

Origin of Pragmatism

Historically, the Pragmatic approach can be traced to '*Protagorus*, a Sophist philosopher of ancient Greece who said, "Man is the Measure of All Things". In recent times the term first appeared in 1878 in "How to Make our Ideas Clear", an article written by C.S. Pierce. He preferred to use the term "Pragmaticism". He attacked idealism and redefined truth and knowledge in terms of experience and their practical consequences. William James developed this outlook out of the American cultural milieu and became the founder and father of this, what Archie J. Bahm calls, 'down to earth' cash-value philosophy. John Dewey (1859-1952) became its leading and most influential exponent. He practised it in his laboratory school set up in Chicago in 1896. His purpose was to train pupils in cooperation and mutually useful living.

Definition of Pragmatism

1. *Will Durant* sums up the meaning and concept of pragmatism as, "Pragmatism is the doctrine that truth is the practical efficacy of an idea".
2. *William James* defines pragmatism as, "Pragmatism is a temper of mind, an attitude; it is also a theory of the nature of ideas and truth; and finally, it is a theory about reality".
3. *J.B. Prett* states, "Pragmatism offers us a theory of truth of knowledge, and a theory of reality".
4. According to *J.S. Ross*, "Pragmatism is essentially a humanistic philosophy, maintaining that man creates his own values in the course of activity that reality is still in the making and awaits its part of completion from the future, that to an unascertainable extent our truths are manmade products".

5. *Rusk* defines pragmatism as, "Pragmatism is merely a stage in the development of a new idealism—an idealism that will do full justice to reality, reconcile the practical and spiritual values and result as a culture which is the flower of efficiency".
6. *Reid* states, "Pragmatism makes activity, engagement, commitment and encounter its central theme".

***Summing up*:** Pragmatism stands between idealism and materialism—a sort of compromise. Idea or mind is the primary thing in idealism: Matter is at the centre of the universe so far as materialism is concerned. They are in fact the two "antithetical trends" in philosophy. For pragmatism "Experience" is at the centre of the Universe.

Forms of Pragmatism

(1) Humanistic Pragmatism

(2) Experimental Pragmatism

(3) Biological Pragmatism

Humanistic Pragmatism: According to a humanistic pragmatism, "Whatever fulfills our purpose, satisfies our desire, develops our life is true".

Experimental Pragmatism: An experimental pragmatist believes, "Whatever can be experimentally verified is true or that works is true".

Biological Pragmatism: A biologist pragmatist believes, "By this type of pragmatism best is found in the function of thought, in adapting the human organism to its environment".

Chief Promoters of Pragmatism in Modern Times

1. C.B. Pierce (1839-1914 A.D.)
2. William James (1842-1910)
3. John Dewey (1859-1952)

Fundamental Principles of Pragmatism

1. Experience is the central idea in pragmatism. According to *John Dewey*, "Truth is made just as health, wealth and strength are made in the course of experience". It is based on results.
2. William James sees no difference between 'pragmatism' and 'practicalism'. Truth is that which works in institutions. It changes with times.
3. There are no absolute values of life.
4. Action is real and ideas are tools.
5. Man is an active being.
6. Man has the ability to solve his problems.
7. Man solves his problems though the logic of experiments and scientific methods.
8. Knowledge is functional and tentative.
9. Utilitarian aspect is supreme.
10. Past has little value.
11. Present and future are more important.
12. Spiritual character of existence has little significance.
13. Pragmatism rejects all types of authoritarianism whether in government or religion or education.

BROAD FEATURES OF PRAGMATISM IN EDUCATION

1. Education should enable the child to learn new techniques to cope with new situations.
2. Values are created through experimentation.
3. Child learns by doing more than by reflection.
4. Education is a continuous process. Education is a constant reorganising or reconstructing of experience.
5. Educational practices have to be experimental.
6. Curriculum is activity centred.
7. Curriculum is integrated.
8. Moral values cannot be imposed by the elders upon the younger generation.
9. Life situations should be made the basis of education.

10. Education is a social necessity. It is the means by which it renews itself.
11. Suitable environment is needed for the development of the personality of the child.
12. Freedom should be given to the child for the development of his all-round personality.
13. Educational experiments lead to the development of philosophy of education.

Pragmatism and Aims of Education

In the words of *Dewey*, "Education as such has no aim".

According to *Ross*, "The most general aim of education according to pragmatism is just creation of new values; the main task of education is to put the educand into position to develop values for himself". Following are the characteristics of the aims of education according to pragmatism:

1. *No Pre-conceived Aims*: There are no pre-conceived aims of education.
2. *No Fixed Aim*: Aims of education are not final and fixed.
3. *Situations and Aims*: Aims of education arise out of situations.
4. *Adaptation to Environment*: Education should enable an individual to adapt to the environment.
5. *Providing Rich Experiences*: Education should provide more and more purposeful experience.
6. *Social Efficiency*: Dewey lays emphasis on preparing a socially efficient individual.
7. *Making Present Life Rich*: The Pragmatists lay great stress on making the present rich and happy.

Pragmatism and Curriculum

Pragmatism points out the following criteria for curriculum construction.

1. *Principle of Utility*: This is the first concern. The school must provide those experiences that are useful to the

child. The utility aspect requires direct training for the later stage of the school.

2. *Principle of Child's Natural Instincts*: The curriculum should be based on the natural instincts of the child.
3. *Principle of Graded Curriculum*: The curriculum should take into account the successive stages of child's development.
4. *Principle of Child's Occupations and Activities*: Curriculum attaches limited importance to book learning. Besides the subjects, the curriculum includes purposive, productive and socialised activities.
5. *Principle of Integration*: Subjects are not treated in water-tight compartments. Subjects are presented as modes of activities. Integration, for the pragmatist is of life, with activity of the learner.
6. *Principle of Social Worth*: A pragmatist also recognises that the subjects and experiences provided to the child must make him socially useful.
7. *Principle of Dynamism*: The pragmatist does not believe in the rigidity of the curriculum. So the curriculum is not static. Curriculum changes according to the needs of the pupils and the society. The main aim of knowledge, i.e., human progress should not be overlooked.

Curriculum includes tools of knowledge as reading, writing, counting, nature study, drawing, handwork, hygiene, physical training, history, geography, science—domestic science for girls and agricultural sciences for boys. Vocational training is an indispensable part of the curriculum.

Pragmatism and Methods of Teaching

The basic principle of education is that child is ever active—doing, doing and doing. While doing, he is learning. While learning, he is doing.

Pragmatism tells us to confront the child with real situations—help him to adjust himself, not by a passive surrender but by a constant, dynamic interaction between himself and the changing situations, himself also changing all the while, for the improvement involves a change in himself. Doing and learning; learning by doing, let him have a perception of 'self'. Let him project himself into a self which he would like to do. Let him strive, struggle, change the situation, change his self and achieve, thus realising his 'self'. All knowledge, all experiences are to be coordinated in human terms. All principles are just pointers.

Child's activities are:

1. Spontaneous activities.
2. Purposeful activities.
3. Socialised activities.

Following are the important principles of pragmatism:

1. Principle of purpose
2. Principle of learning by doing
3. Principle of integration
4. Principle of project or project method

Pragmatism and Discipline

Pragmatism holds that discipline should be social through and through. Free, purposeful and cooperative activities organised in the school lead to social discipline. These activities inculcate attitudes of cooperation and consideration. Besides, these keep the students busy in worthwhile tasks. Moral development taken place through such activities. Students develop a sense of self-control.

Pragmatism and the Teacher

Pragmatism regards the teacher as a helper and guide. The teacher assumes the role of an 'arranger of experience'. According to Dewey, "The teacher is a guide and director, he steers the boat, but the energy that propels it must come from those who are learning".

The teacher's job is to keep the child alive to:

His purposes,
His capacities,
His limitations.

So that he evolves his own discipline.

Develops his own values,
Makes his own adjustment,
And thus realises himself.

Pragmatism and the School

Dewey regarded the school as an 'epitome' of life outside, as the 'miniature of society' and also the 'lengthened arm of the family'.

Dewey sets out the following functions of the school.

1. *Providing a Simplified Environment*: A complex civilisation is too complex to be assimilated in toto. It has to be broken up into portions, and assimilated in a gradual and graded way. The relationships of our present social life are so numerous and so inter-woven that even a child placed in the most favourable position could not readily share in many of the most important of them. The first function of the school, therefore, is to select those features which are fairly fundamental and capable of being responded to by the young.

2. *Eliminating 'the Unworthy Features of the Existing Environment'*: Dewey explains this point, "As a society becomes more enlightened, it realises that it is responsible not to transmit and conserve the whole of its existing achievements but only such as make for a better future society. The school is the chief agency for the accomplishment of this end."

3. *Balancing the Various Elements in the Social Environment*: It is the function of the school to co-ordinate within the disposition of each individual the diverse influences of the various social environments into which he enters.

That education which does not occur through forms of life, forms that are worth living for their own sake, is always a poor substitute for the genuine reality, and tends to cramp and to deaden.

The school, as an institution, should simplify existing social life; should reduce it, as it were, to an embryonic form. Existing life is so complex that the child cannot be brought into contact with it without either confusion or distraction; he is either overwhelmed by the multiplicity of activities which are going on, so that he loses his own power of orderly reaction, or he is so stimulated by these various activities that his powers are prematurely called into play and he becomes either unduly specialised or else disintegrated.

The social life of the child is the basis of concentration or correlation, in all his training or growth. The social life gives the unconscious unity and the background of all his attainments.

The subject-matter of the school curriculum should mark a gradual differentiation out of the primitive unconscious unity of social life.

We violate the child's nature and render difficult the best ethical results by introducing the child too abruptly to a number of special studies, of reading, writing, geography, etc. out of relation to this social life.

The true centre of correlation on the school subject is not science, nor literature, nor history, nor geography but the child's own social activities.

The studies represent the possibilities of development inherent in the child's immediate crude experience.

Following are the important features of a school:

1. School as an enlarged ideal home.
2. School as a society in miniature.
3. School as a child centred institution.
4. School as a place of providing rich experiences.
5. School as a provider of vocational training.
6. School as a place of training socially efficient individuals.
7. School as a place of 'learning by doing'.
8. School as a place where learning takes place through projects.
9. School as a place of discipline through co-curriculum activities and social environment.
10. School as a place where teacher plays the role of a friend, philosopher and guide.

LIMITATIONS OF PRAGMATISM

1. *Ignoring Eternal Values*: Pragmatism, by and large, ignores eternal values.
2. *Ignoring Spiritual Values*: Pragmatism pays little attention to spiritual values.
3. *Over Emphasis on Material Values*: Pragmatism lays too much emphasis on material things.
4. *Utilitarian Approach*: Pragmatism advocates a utilitarian approach only.
5. *Ignoring Cultural Values*: Pragmatism provides very insignificant place to cultural values.
6. *Neglect of Cultural Heritage*: Pragmatism believes that experience is all in all. It ignores the knowledge accumulated through the ages.
7. *Neglect of System*: Pragmatism does not give due importance to regular and systematic instruction.
8. *Limitations of Projects*: The entire knowledge and experience needed by the child cannot be obtained through projects.
9. *Heavy Demand of the Teacher*: Pragmatism places heavy demands on the teacher.
10. *No Fixed Goals*: Pragmatism does not indicate fixed educational goals.

CONTRIBUTION OF PRAGMATISM TO EDUCATION

1. *Freeing the Over Burdened Child*: Pragmatism saves the child from the burden of education which is too much centred on books.
2. *Due Emphasis on Experience*: Pragmatism helps us in realising the value of today's life by experiencing it.
3. *Balanced Approach*: Pragmatism advises us to have a balanced approach towards the past, present and future. The past may be glorious and rich but it must guide for living a glorious and rich life in the present. Thus too much emphasis on cultural heritage should not be laid.

4. *Learning How to Learn*: The focus of the teaching-learning process is to enable the child how to learn.
5. *Inflexible Methods*: Methods of teaching are based on utility and fulfilment the demands of the society.
6. *Group Methods*: Pragmatism advocates that children should get real experience of group life.
7. *Correlated Methods*: Pragmatism stresses that in order to make progressive methods of teaching successful and effective, there is the need of correlation of studies, integration of subjects, use of audio-visual aids, organisation of curriculum activities, learning by doing, direct experience and proper training of senses.
8. *Developing Self-effort*: Pragmatism believes in developing self-effort.
9. *Group Method for Moral Education*: Pragmatism envisages that the method of moral education should be through group life.
10. *Project Method*: Project method is the most important contribution of pragmatism.
11. *Experience and More Experience*: Pragmatism believes in experimenting with new methods.
12. *Pragmatism Against Bookish Knowledge*: Pragmatism lays stress on action rather than reflection. The child does not learn much from books. He learns from his own experiences, new situations and activities. Pragmatism, therefore, enjoins upon the teaching maxim, 'learning by doing'. Practical work is a very important means of instruction. The child should be put in real situations so that he may himself solve the problems arising out of them.
13. *Social Discipline*: Pragmatism accords a special role to activities leading to social discipline.
14. *Balanced Approach to the Role of the Teacher and the Pupil*: Pragmatism accepts that the teacher and the students are the active participants in the educative process.

COMPARATIVE IMPACT OF IDEALISM, NATURALISM AND PRAGMATISM ON EDUCATIONAL THEORY AND PRACTICE

Idealism	*Naturalism*	*Pragmatism*
I. *Basic Philosophical Features*		
1. Idealism believes in the existence of God.	1. Naturalism has no belief in the existence of God.	1. Pragmatism has some belief in the existence of God.
2. Universe is God's creation.	2. Universe is man's creation.	2. Universe is natural creation.
3. Ultimate reality is spiritual.	3. Ultimate reality is physical.	3. Ultimate reality is utility.
4. Eternal spiritual values never change.	4. Values are not eternal.	4. Values are changeable.
5. Truth, beauty and goodness are eternal values.	5. There are no such values.	5. The nature of these values undergoes changes.
6. Spiritual laws are universal	6. Physical and natural laws are universal	6. There are no universal laws
II. *Aims of Education*		
1. Self-realisation aim.	1. Self-expression aim.	1. Self-sufficiency aim.
2. Spiritual development aim.	2. Autonomous development of the individuality aim.	2. Adjustment with present aim.
3. Character development aim.	3. Adjustment to environment aim.	

(Contd.)

Idealism	*Naturalism*	*Pragmatism*
III. *Curriculum*		
1. Emphasis on ethics and humanities. 2. Study of cultural heritage.	1. Emphasis on sciences. 2. Curriculum band on the need, ability and aptitude of the individual nature.	1. Stress on utilitarian subjects and vocational subjects, 2. Life experiences. 3. Integrated curriculum
IV. *Methods of Teaching*		
1. Lecture method. 2. Question-answer method.	1. Direct observation. 2. Heuristic method.	1. Learning by doing. 2. Project method.
V. *Discipline*		
1. Emphasis on regulated freedom. 2. Self discipline.	1. Uncontrolled freedom. 2. Discipline through natural consequences.	1. Social discipline. 2. Discipline through group work.
VI. *Teacher's Role*		
1. Important role of the teacher. 2. Importance of teacher's personality. 3. Teacher as an ideal person.	1. Limited role of the teacher. 2. Very little importance to teacher's personality. 3. Teacher as an observer.	1. Teacher as a guide. 2. Limited importance. 3. Teacher as a friend and philosopher.

Rusk explains the difference in these philosophies as "Naturalism reduces everything to life, idealism to mind or spirit and pragmatism sees no necessity for seeking one fundamental principle of explanation. It is quite content to admit several principles and accordingly is pluralistic".

According to *William James*, "For naturalisms reality is ready-made and complete, while for pragmatist, it is still in the making and awaits its part of completion from the future".

Summing up: We cannot remain wedded to a particular philosophy. Each philosophy contributes something to educational theory and practice. We must make a balanced and rational use of each type of philosophy according to needs.

6

Rousseau (1712-1778)

A BRIEF LIFE SKETCH

Rousseau, a great Swiss political thinker and educational reformer lost his father at an early age. His father was a poor watchman and could not provide him regular schooling. He left school at the age of 12 and tried unsuccessfully all sorts of occupations – apprenticeship to an engraver etc. He became a music critic for sometimes at Paris. From the age of twelve to twenty nine years, he remained a vagabond and during his wanderings he met different types of people, learnt to sympathise with the poor. He developed love for nature. He also defied the conventional rules of society.

Rousseau revolted against the established (canons) of society and advocated the doctrine of "Back to nature". He wrote, "Man is born free and every where he is in chains". His ideas were vehemently opposed by the establishment. His books were burnt. He incurred the displeasure of the French authorities and had to live in exile for many years. He was so much disgusted and disappointed that he committed suicide in 1778. However, his greatness was recognised later on and his views had tremendous influence on the outbreak of the French Revolution in 1789.

PUBLICATIONS OF ROUSSEAU AND ESSENCE OF HIS WRITINGS

After wandering for a number of years, he settled down in Paris (France). In 1750, at the age of 38, Rousseau wrote his first book *The Progress of the Art and the Science*. This was followed by *The Origin of Inequality Among Men* (1753), *The New Heloise – A Romance* (1759); *Social Contract* (1762), and *Emile* or *Concerning Education* (1762).

In his publications, he criticised the existing institutions. He attributed the existing oppression and corruption of the society to the advancement of civilisation which according to him was the main cause of the differences and inequalities among men. Regarding the absolute powers of the sovereign, Rousseau wrote, "He cannot impose upon his subjects fetters that are useless to the community".

ROUSSEAU'S VIEWS ON EDUCATIONAL THEORY AND PRACTICES

I. Rousseau's Educational Philosophy

'Return to nature' was the theme of his two educational publications (novels): *The New Heloise* (1761) and '*Emile*' (1762). These books, were among the most widely read of the popular writing of the century.

Rousseau was an arch enemy of child neglect. His *Emile* made Europe child conscious. It is still widely quoted in almost all books on educational philosophy: principles and practices.

II. Sources of Education

According to Rousseau following are the three main sources of education.

1. *Education of Nature*: "The constitutional exertion of our organs and faculties is the education of nature".

2. *Education given by Men*: "The uses we are taught to make of that exertion, constitute the education given to us by men".

3. *Education from Circumstances*: "And in the acquisition made by our own experience, on the objects that surround us, consists our education from circumstances".

By education from nature, he meant development according to the child's endowments and capacities. By education from men, he emphasised the importance of social environment, teaching how to make use of that development. By education from things, he understood physical environment, helping to gain experience by ourselves. He says that harmonious development of these three factors constitutes an ideal scheme of education.

Such harmony in education is possible by subordinating the education of men and things to that of nature because we have no control over nature. We, must, therefore, direct the other two, to ensure cooperation of these factors for imparting ideal education.

III. Rousseau's Theory of Negative Education

Rousseau believed that everything is good as it comes from nature and it generates in the hands of man, so he advocated that the education of the child should be purely negative. The child should not be taught the principles of truth and virtue but guarded against evil. He wrote, "I call a positive education one that tends to form the mind prematurely and to instruct the child in the duties that belong to him. I call negative education one that tends to perfect the organs that are the instruments of knowledge and endeavours to process the way for reasons, by the proper exercises of senses".

IV. Aims of Education

Rousseau's aim of education was the attainment of fullest natural growth of the individual, leading to balanced, harmonious useful and natural life. The real aim of education is to help the child to live his life. He says, "To live is not merely to breathe. It is to act, to make use of our organs, senses, our faculties and of all those parts of ourselves, which give us the feeling of our existence".

This general aim of education was split up by Rousseau, according to the nature, at different stages of human development.

(i) *Infancy*, i.e., from birth to the age of five years, the aim of education is to develop a well-regulated freedom.

(ii) *In childhood*, i.e., between the age of five and twelve, the main aim of education is to provide the child with the strength which he needs for the attainment of well-regulated freedom.

(iii) *In boyhood or pre-adolescent period*, i.e., from twelve years to fifteen years the aim of education is "to acquire such knowledge which may satisfy the wants of the child and must be functionally useful". This is the period for intellectual education—the period of instruction, labour and study.

(iv) *In adolescent period*, i.e., from 15 to 20 years, the aim of education is the training of heart, to make the child loving and tender-hearted so that he may live peacefully in social relationship. In this period, religious, moral and social education is recommended. In the previous periods, the child has already developed physically and intellectually. He must now grow emotionally, aesthetically, socially and morally. The sex instinct, which is sufficiently developed by this time, is to be sublimated by re-directing it to the love of some noble idea and by keeping the young occupied in work and activity.

V. Curriculum

Rousseau recommends curriculum in accordance with the nature of each stage of the child.

Curriculum at the First Stage: Curriculum at the first stage (from one to 5 years) would be such as it develops physical strength. The child should be allowed to wander freely on the country-side. His play-things should be very simple such as branches with fruits and flowers and no expensive toys. 'Let him not be pampered! Let him not be subdued'.

Curriculum at the Second Stage: Curriculum at the second stage (between 5 to 12 years) should lead to the development of senses. Rousseau thinks that if senses are not trained properly, independent reasoning and judgement are impossible. Emile (the hero of the novel Emile) is to be given the greatest freedom of physical movement, simple diet and light clothing. There will be no verbal lessons for him. He will not be instructed in language, history and geography. Emile is to learn from his own experience. No moral instruction is to be given. "Exercise the body, the organs, the senses and powers but keep the soul lying fallow as long as you can." Training for senses means learning to judge, foresee and reason through them. It is more than the mere use of them. All learning must come by play-way. There is no need for the child to learn anything by heart. For Emile there is no curriculum. He has to learn by activity and experience.

Curriculum at the Third Stage: Curriculum at the third stage of pre-adolescence (12 to 15 years) should be built around curiosity which should create an urge for knowledge. Rousseau states that this is the period for developing intellect. Emile is introduced to studies that reveal nature, astronomy, science and the arts and crafts. Rousseau emphasises the learning of manual and industrial arts partly to make Emile independent and partly to overcome the prejudice held against the manual work. Rousseau wanted that the boy must be taken from one workshop to another and he must try his hand at every trade. In this way Rousseau wanted to teach him industrial exchange, banking and transportation. Rousseau does not recommend the study of books. The only book he recommends is *Robinson Crusoe*, a study of life according to nature.

Curriculum at the Fourth Stage: In the fourth stage of the adolescence period (15 to 20 years of age), training of heart should receive attention. In the earlier stages, the boy was an individual working for self-perfection and self-development. Now he has to be social and adapt himself to the conduct and interest of others. The study of society, politics, economics, history and religion are the appropriate studies for the youth to understand complex social relationships. Emile must be provided opportunities for training in moral education about his relations with his fellow men and moral qualities such as benevolence, kindness, service and sympathy. Rousseau recommends that moral education should be given through activities and occupations and not through lectures on ethics. History will be utilised as a means of moral instruction. Travel is recommended for knowing the world and the institutions of the neighbouring countries. At this stage the youth undergoes a new birth on account of the appearance of sex impulse. Sex instruction is to consist of direct moral exhortation on chastity and an explanation of the mysteries of creation in the world of plants, animals and men in a dispassionate manner.

Education of Women: Rousseau maintained that women were the makers of men. They were, "the chaste guardians of our morals, and the sweet security of our place". Their education was to be different from men. Rousseau believed that "Woman is made specially to please man". She has, therefore, to be taught to be soft and sweet and learn to suffer and bear the wrongs of her husband without complaint". The duty of women towards man is "to train him in childhood, to tend him in womanhood, and to counsel him throughout his life". Rousseau, therefore, advocated that her studies, should be practical. Intellectual interests, he believed, destroyed her nature. He stated, "I would a hundred times prefer a simple girl, rudely brought up to a girl of learning".

He remarked, "A woman of literacy education (culture) is the plague of her husband; her children, her family, her servants—everybody". Sophie, therefore, is to learn embroidery, lace making, the art of house decorating and house keeping, sewing etc.

VI. Methods of Teaching

Observation of the Nature of the Child: Rousseau wrote, "I wish some discreet person would give us a treatise on the art of observing children—an art which would be of immense value to us but of which parents and schoolmasters have not yet learnt the very first rudiment".

Art of Teaching: Rousseau further said, "To know how to suggest is the art of teaching".

Rousseau emphasised, "The highest function of the teacher consists not much in imparting knowledge as in stimulating the pupil in its love and pursuit".

He was against the harsh and unsympathetic methods of education which repressed the natural inclinations and tendencies of the child. He advocated simple and direct methods of instruction and urged, "experience before expression" and "objects before words". He said, "Give your scholar no verbal lesson. He should be taught by experience alone. Teach by doing whenever you can and only fall back upon words when doing is out of question. Book knowledge should be as little as possible". Emphasising "object teaching", he remarked, "Let the senses always be the guides. Let there be no books but the world and no other instruction than facts. The child who reads, does not think, he merely reads. He is not receiving instruction but learning words".

Methods of teaching advocated by Rousseau may be summed as:

1. Do not teach books. "I hate books. They only teach us to talk about things that we know nothing about. To conceal their deficiencies, teachers choose the dead languages—words, words, words".
2. Provide opportunities to children from their own experience and not from books.
   "Let him (the child) not be taught science, let him discover it".
3. Provide sense training.
4. Never substitute the symbol for the thing unless it is impossible to show the thing itself.

VII. Role of the Teacher

Rousseau assigns a minor place to the teacher in the educative process. He is not called an instructor but only a guide.

His main responsibility is to motivate the child to learn. This he can achieve by exploiting the innate tendencies of the child. He must possess a profound understanding of the child's nature and be able to control his emotional reactions. He is not to impose any rules of control upon the child. He is to allow him perfect freedom and guide him properly.

Rousseau wrote, "The highest function of the teacher consists not so much in imparting knowledge as on stimulating the pupil in its love and pursuit". Further he advises, "To know how to suggest is the art of teaching". Rousseau placed stress on developing the reasoning power of the child. He observed, "If ever you (teacher) substitute authority in the place of argument, he (child) will reason no longer, he will ever afterwards be handed like a shuttle cork between the opinion of others".

VIII. Freedom of the Child—Discipline by Natural Consequences

He believes in freedom of the child. It is only in a free atmosphere that the child will be able to develop his inborn and innate capacities. He does not believe in punishing the child so as to correct his future behaviour. The reason behind this assumption according to Rousseau is very simple—the child is not able to link up the punishment administered and the mischief done by him. Children, therefore, should be left alone to experience the consequences of the mischief done by them. Nature, according to Rousseau, is a great teacher. If children commit mistakes and violate the principles of nature, they naturally invite the retribution of nature. This conception in the field of education is known as "Discipline by natural consequences".

Secondly, in the field of education, Rousseau starts with the assumption that the nature of child is essentially good, hence he should have freedom in his actions. Firstly he believes that the child will not commit any immoral act, and secondly even if he commits any, he will learn morality by the natural consequences of the action done.

'EMILE': AN IMPORTANT TREATISE ON EDUCATION

Emile is a treatise on education cast in the form of a novel in which there are three characters; Emile, who may be regarded as 'Rousseau' while a boy, and his tutor, who is obviously Rousseau, as a man, Sophie, who is destined to be the mate of Emile.

Emile consists of five books or parts on training and education.

Book I deals with the infant; Book II with childhood; Book III with the pre-adolescent between the ages of twelve and fifteen; Book IV with adolescence; and Book V with the education of girls.

(Curriculum given in *Emile* has been detailed above)

Lord Morley has described the value of *Emile* in these words, "It touched the deeper things of character. It filled parents with a sense of the dignity of their task. It cleared away the accumulation of clogging prejudices and obscure inveterate usage, which made education one of the dark formalistic arts. It admitted floods of light and air into the tightly closed nurseries and school rooms. It effected the substitution of growth for mechanism... It was the charter of youthful deliverance".

On the other hand, the Parliament of Paris criticised *Emile* very severely. It was ordered to be burnt publicly. Orders for the arrest of Rousseau were issued and he had to run away from France to Switzerland. The reading of *Emile* was forbidden by the Archbishop of Paris. The book was condemned on account of 'Containing an abominable doctrine, ready to subvert natural law and to destroy the foundations of the Christian religion... tending to trouble the peace of States, to cause subjects to revolt against their sovereigns; as containing a large number of prepositions false, scandalous, full of hate against the Church, derogatory to the respect of holy scriptures .... erroneous, impious, blasphemous and heretical".

AN ANALYSIS OF ROUSSEAU'S VIEWS ON EDUCATION

1. Rousseau has not suggested a formal system of education.
2. Physical nature alone is not sufficient for providing education.
3. Rousseau almost ignores the importance of books and other media. It is difficult to assume that we can neglect the vast intellectual heritage.
4. Absolute freedom as recommended by Rousseau is a myth. It cannot exist. It never existed and will not exist. We cannot allow the child to hang himself from a long rope—punishment by natural consequences. We cannot allow the child to have a taste of poison and suffer the natural consequences of his action.
5. Rousseau does not give due importance to the role of the teacher in the education of the child.
6. It is very difficult to find naturalistic surroundings to locate educational institutions.
7. Rousseau's ideas about the role and education of women are very conservative and do not appeal to the modern mind.
8. Rousseau's educational principles are the outcome of his theorising. These were not put to test in any realistic educational setting.

ROUSSEAU'S CONTRIBUTION TO EDUCATION

Notwithstanding some limitations, Rousseau stands to modern education as Plato to ancient education. His *Emile* made Europe child conscious so much as no writing had done for centuries and it became an inspiring source of reforms. William Boyd in *History of Western Education* has paid glowing tribute to *Emile*. "Judged by effects on thought and action is indeed perhaps the most considerable book ever written on education"

Rousseau's chief contributions may be summarised as:

1. Rousseau was the fore-runner of the modern educational psychology. He ushered in a new movement in education by emphasising the importance of individual differences.
2. He laid stress on the spontaneous unfolding of child's capacities.
3. He pointed out the importance of observing the natural traits of children.
4. He stressed that in the drama of education, child must play the role of the 'hero' and all actors subordinate roles.
5. He propounded the idea of 'learning by doing'.

Opportunistic, unreliable, unscrupulous, at times, a gigolo, at other times a liar, a thief and the unacknowledged father of several illegitimate children by his own confession, Rousseau had the flash of a genius that seemed to attract followers and friends despite his shortcomings. His writings have exercised such an influence on educational theory and practice that they are widely quoted even today. There is no doubt that he is considered one of the great leaders of the world.

7

Dewey, John (1852-1959)

BRIEF LIFE SKETCH OF JOHN DEWEY

Dewey was born in 1859 at Burlington in the USA. He graduated from the University of Vermont in 1879 and started his career as a teacher. Thereafter he joined Hopkins University and obtained his Ph.D. degree in Philosophy in 1884. He worked as a Professor of Philosophy at the University of Minnesota, Michigan and Chicago. His last assignment was his professorship of education and philosophy at the University of Columbia, New York.

Prof. Dewey delivered lectures on education and philosophy at the University of Peking for a period of two years.

The Government of Turkey invited Dewey to draw up a report on the reorganisation of national schools.

Prof. Dewey's philosophy is not simply speculative but based on actual experiences in the classroom. His principles and practices grew out of his experiments in the University Laboratory School, Chicago. He founded this school in 1896, for the chief objective of testing educational theory through experiments.

PUBLICATIONS OF JOHN DEWEY

Perhaps no educator has written such a standard and diverse literature on educational principles and practices as Prof. Dewey. Likewise enormous material has been published on him and his works. His first article entitled 'The Metaphysical Assumption of Materialism' appeared in Journal of Speculative Philosophy in April 1882.

Dewey's important publications are as under:

1. *My Pedagogic Creed* (1897)
2. *Psychology and Philosophic Method* (1899)
3. *Studies in Logical Theory* (1903)
4. *Ethics* (1908)
5. *The Influence of Darwin and Other Essays* (1910)
6. *How We Think* (1910)
7. *Democracy and Education* (1916)
8. *Essays in Experimental Logic* (1916)
9. *Creative Intelligence* (1917)
10. *Lectures at Tokyo Imperial University* (1920)
11. *Reconstruction in Philosophy* (1920)
12. *Human Nature and Conduct* (1922)
13. *Experience and Nature* (1925)
14. *The Public and Its Problem* (1927)
15. *The Quest for Certainty* (1927)
16. *Art as Experience* (1934)
17. *A Common Faith* (1934)
18. *Philosophy and Civilisation* (1934)
19. *Liberalism and Social Action* (1935)
20. *Experience in Education* (1938)
21. *Freedom and Culture* (1939)
22. *Theory of Valuation* (1939)
23. *Problems of Men* (1946)
24. *Knowing and the Known* (1949)
25. *Education Today* (1949)
26. *Interest and Effort in Education* (1953)
27. *Schools of Tomorrow* (1953)
28. *The Child and the Curriculum* (1956)
29. *The School and Society* (1900)
30. *Philosophy of Education* (1958)
31. *Moral Principles in Education* (1959)

DEWEY'S VIEWS ON VARIOUS ASPECTS OF EDUCATION

1. Dewey's Philosophy of Education

Dewey's philosophy of education is given various names. 'Experimentalism', 'Functionalism', 'Instrumentalism', 'Operationalism', 'Practicalism', 'Pragmatism' and 'Progressivism'. Of course, his philosophy of education is mostly associated with the term 'Pragmatism'. All these terms indicate the dynamic, ever-changing and performing character of life. Dewey suggested the application of experimental logic. He emphasised that as all experiences cannot be educative, the business of the educator is to select an experience or experiences which would enable the individuals to live creatively, constructively, dynamically and fruitfully in the changing environment.

What is a thing for? What is its use? Action must precede knowledge. Whatever knowledge we possess has resulted from our activities, our efforts to survive. Only that which has been organised into our dispositions so as to enable us to adapt our environment to our needs and to adapt our aims and desires to the situations in which we exist is really knowledge.

2. Meaning of Education

Education as a Psychological and Social Process: Dewey does not believe in absolute values. According to Dewey, "Education is the process of reconstruction or reconstitution of experience, giving it a more detailed value through the medium of increased social efficiency". Dewey further observed, "What nutrition and reproduction are to physiological life, education is to social life". He considered education as 'the fundamental method of social progress and reform. In sum, I believe that the individual who is to be educated is a social individual and that society is an organic union of individuals. If we eliminate the social factor from the child, we are left only with an abstraction; if we eliminate the individual factor from society, we are left only with an inert and lifeless mass. Education, therefore, must begin with a psychological insight into the child's capacities, interests, and habits. It must be controlled at every point by reference to these same considerations. These powers, interests, and habits must be continually interpreted – we must know what they mean. They must be translated in terms of their social equivalents in terms of what they are capable of in the way of social service'.

"I believe that all education proceeds by the participation of the individual in the social consciousness of the race. This process begins unconsciously almost at birth, and is continually shaping the individual's powers, saturating his consciousness, forming his habits, training his ideas, and arousing his feelings and emotions. Through this unconscious education the individual gradually comes to share in the intellectual and moral resources which humanity has succeeded in getting together. He becomes an inheritor of the funded capital of civilisation. The most formal and technical education in the world cannot safely depart from this general process. It can only organise it or differentiate it in some particular direction.

I believe that the only true education comes through the stimulation of the child's powers by the demands of the social situations in which he finds himself."

3. Dewey's Concept of Social Efficiency

Social efficiency broadly speaking includes three elements of efficient industrial development and the art of living together. A man must learn to be economically self-sufficient and at the same time acquire qualities and values of an enlightened citizen. An individual must be able to earn his livelihood. An individual who is not able to earn his livelihood, is a parasite. Education must take into account economic aspect. An individual should be trained to make the best use of national resources. A school was considered as a 'society in miniature'.

Dewey was a firm believer in democratic values. He, therefore, insisted that education should provide suitable opportunities to the students to imbibe democratic values.

4. Functions of Education

Dewey explains the functions of education in these words, "It is a common place to say that development of character is the ultimate end of all school work. In general, character means organised capacity of social functioning. It means social interest and responsiveness". He further says, "The function of education is to help the growing of a helpless young animal into a happy, moral and efficient human being".

5. Child's Place in the Educative Process

Dewey observes, "Education must begin with a psychological insight into the child's capacities, interests and habits. These must be continually interpreted, we must know what they mean. They must be translated into their social equivalents—into terms of what they are capable of in the way of social service". In this regard he outlined the function of the teacher as, "The more a teacher is aware of the past experience of students, of their hopes, desires, chief interests, the better will he understand the forces at work that need to be directed and utilised for the formation of reflective habits."

6. Curriculum

The curriculum must grow out of child's interests, experiences, impulses and needs. The curriculum must be child-centred. He stressed that the school subjects should be woven around the child's activities. Lessons should begin with social topics such as food, shelter, modes of communication, speech, reading, drawing, modelling, etc. While laying stress on the needs of the children, Dewey also took into account the needs of the community in which the children live.

Following are the main characteristics and principles of the curriculum:

1. Curriculum should reflect the social life and social activities. It should have utility.

2. It must follow the principle of progressive organisation of knowledge consisting of educative experiences and problems of the learners.
3. The new experiences and problems should grow out of the old ones.
4. The experiences should be flexible and changeable in accordance with the child's interests and should be graded.

7. Methods of Teaching

Dewey said, "All learning must come as a by-product of actions and for its own sake". This reveals his concepts of observation, and direct experience. According to him, a child learns through participation in various activities. He advocated 'learning by doing' and 'learning by living'. He recommended the Project Method which is based on problems, activities, experiments and interests of the learners.

Dewey has explained the problem method of teaching in his books: *How We Think* and *Interest and Effort in Education* as, "the processes by which the mind of the individual comes into relation with the objective world. Interest and self-activity are the characteristic features". It is a method which deals with the intellectual processes that are antecedent to induction and deduction.

Dewey briefly recommended the following methods of instruction:

1. Learning by doing.
2. Learning by integration and correlation.
3. Learning through productive and creative activities.

8. Dewey's Concept of Discipline

Dewey held that the natural impulses of the child ought to be directed and disciplined through the cooperative activities of the school. "Out of doing things that are to produce results, and out of doing in a social and cooperative way, there is born a discipline of its own kind and type". Dewey believed that the child's activities – intellectual, social, moral and physical – are disciplinary in their effect if they are carried out in cooperation with others.

9. John Dewey on the Role of the Teacher

The teacher is engaged not simply in the training of individuals, but in the formation of the proper social life.

Every teacher should realise the dignity of his calling; that he is a social servant set apart for the maintenance of proper social order and the securing of the right social growth.

In this way the teacher always is the 'prophet of the true God' and the usherer in the true kingdom of God. He also said, "The teacher is a guide and director; he steers the boat, but the energy that propels it must come from those who are learning. The more a teacher is aware of the past experiences of students, of their hopes, desires, chief interests, the better will he understand the forces at work that need to be directed and utilised for the formation of reflective habits".

10. Dewey's Concept of Democracy and Democratic Values in Education

Dewey states that democracy is the political and moral philosophy of education. "If education is equivalent to genuine living, then democracy is the moral foundation of education. The essence of education is the extension of shared areas of meaningful action and this is also the essence of democracy".

The school as the 'democratic society in miniature' should provide for the participation of the students in the activities of the school on the one hand and on the other hand it should realise the significance of the experiences, needs and interests of the child as a personality.

Democracy postulates full freedom of enquiry into social and political problems and solving them. Likewise the schools should promote a spirit of enquiry in educational thinking. Discussion should be freely permitted.

The schools should become guardians of academic freedom. Intellectual or moral freedom is the basis of political freedom.

The schools should become living examples of the practices of freedom of enquiry, experimentation and intelligent communication.

Excessive heavy routines and rules are not conducive to self and social disciplines.

Dewey advocates that teacher should be provided opportunities to "participate in the formation of the controlling aims, methods and materials of the school of which he is apart".

To sum up, Dewey wants that education should reflect democratic principles and practices in matters of school organisation, selection of activities and experiences and other matters.

FUNCTIONS OF THE SCHOOL: SCHOOL RELATED TO SOCIAL LIFE

Dewey regarded school as the 'epitome' of life outside, as the 'miniature society' and also the 'lengthened arm of the family'. He said, "The school, now divorced from life, must be reunited with it through activities that will simplify its relations, develop its essential meaning, eliminate its unworthy and obsolescent features, and extend the individual's social environment so that he escapes from the limitations of the group into which he is born".

Dewey sets out the following functions of the school.

1. *Providing a Simplified Environment*: A complex civilisation is too complex to be assimilated in toto. It has to be broken up into portions, and assimilated in a gradual and graded way. The relationships of our present social life are so numerous and so inter-woven that even a child placed in the most favourable position could not readily share in many of the most important of them. The first function of the school, therefore, is to select those features which are fairly fundamental and capable of being responded to by the young.

2. *Eliminating 'the Unworthy Features of the Existing Environment'*: Dewey explains this point, "As a society becomes more enlightened, it realises that it is responsible not to transmit

and conserve the whole of its existing achievements but only such as make for a better future society. The school is the chief agency for the accomplishment of this end".

3. *Balancing the Various Elements in the Social Environment*: It is the function of the school to coordinate within the disposition of each individual the diverse influences of the various social environments into which he enters.

That education which does not occur through forms of life, forms that are worth living for their own sake, is always a poor substitute for the genuine reality, and tends to cramp and to deaden.

The school, as an institution, should simplify existing social life; should reduce it, as it were, to an embryonic form. Existing life is so complex that the child cannot be brought into contact with it without either confusion or distraction; he is either overwhelmed by the multiplicity of activities which are going on, so that he loses his own power of orderly reaction, or he is so stimulated by these various activities that his powers are prematurely called into play and he becomes either unduly specialised or else disintegrated.

The social life of the child is the basis of concentration or correlation, in all his training or growth. The social life gives the unconscious unity and the background of all his attainments.

The subject-matter of the school curriculum should mark a gradual differentiation out of the primitive unconscious unity of social life.

We violate the child's nature and render difficult the best ethical results by introducing the child too abruptly to a number of special studies, of reading, writing, geography, etc. out of relation to this social life.

The true centre of correlation on the school subject is not science, nor literature, nor history, nor geography but the child's own social activities.

The studies represent the possibilities of development inherent in the child's immediate crude experience.

LABORATORY SCHOOL, UNIVERSITY OF CHICAGO

Objective: Dewey felt that the changed times demanded that the training of students for a complete living in the society should be provided in the school. For finding out the type of training to be imparted, he carried out his experiments in the school which he established in 1896.

Main Problems: Following were the main educational problems which Dewey wanted to solve:

1. How to bring the school into closer relation with the home and surrounding life.
2. How to introduce subject-matter in various disciplines like history, science and art to impart a positive value and real significance in child's life.
3. How can instructions in different subjects be carried on with everyday experience and occupation, as the background and be correlated with each other.
4. How individual powers and needs be catered to.

Manual Occupations as the Basis: Dewey introduced the following manual occupations related to everyday life for imparting knowledge of various subjects:

(i) Shop work with wood and tools.
(ii) Cooking work.
(iii) Work with textiles (sewing and weaving).

Dewey accorded a central place to occupations and other subjects were treated incidentally as ancillary to practical activities. Dewey observed that the students think out how to make cloth and reinvent the carding frame, tool for spinning and understand the loom. They learn at the same time enough art and science. "Make the construction adequate, make it full, free and flexible, give it a social motive, something to tell and you have a work of art". Likewise the knowledge of various subjects revolves round such occupations.

Graded Curriculum. Development of interests through occupations was to take place in a developing sequence in accordance with the mental development of the child. Elementary school life was divided into the following periods.

1. Play Period (4 to 8 years of age).
2. Period of Spontaneous Attention (8 to 12 years of age).
3. Period of Affective Attention (12 years onwards).

In the elementary school, the curriculum is based on the four-fold interest of the child.

(a) Interest in conversation and communication.
(b) Interest in inquiry.
(c) Interest in making things or construction.
(d) interest in artistic expression.

ESSENCE OF JOHN DEWEY'S WORK: CONTRIBUTION TO EDUCATION

1. Dewey fused both the psychological and sociological aspects of education.
2. Dewey emphasised democratic values in all dimensions of education.
3. Dewey laid stress on providing rich and varied activities and experiences to students.
4. Dewey's approach to methodology of teaching led to the emergence of the Project Method in education.
5. Dewey advocated that the programmes of the school should be linked with the life of the society. He in this regard, pointed out that the activities should be simplified and that unworthy activities should be discarded.
6. Dewey wanted that the natural interests of the child should be given due attention.
7. Dewey believed in social discipline that could develop through useful activities.

8. Dewey's watchword was social efficiency coupled with individual efficiency.

EVALUATION OF DEWEY'S WORK

Following points of criticism are usually made:

1. Dewey does not suggest any definite aim of education.
2. Dewey attaches more importance to materialism.
3. Dewey does not accept any truth as something permanent.
4. Dewey puts excessive emphasis on individual differences.
5. Dewey lays too much emphasis on experiences.

Prof. V.P. Verma, in *Studies in the Philosophy of Education* (1964) has given the following merits and demerits of Dewey's theory of education.

Merits: (a) It is a 'social' theory of education as opposed to the stress on the isolated self of the individual.

(b) It is a passionate plea for the wide application of the 'experimental' method in education.

(c) It provides the conception of 'democracy' as a social psychological theory of the progressive extension of shared experiences.

Demerits: (a) Dewey's attempt to trace the roots of the dualist approach (two opposed groups of antagonistic interests) – two-fold division of society is a mistake.

(b) Scientific objectivity and veracity may be difficult for being reconciled with democracy, which in practice, means numerical majority.

(c) The neglect of religious education may result in the destruction of the roots of humanistic values and social ethics.

Fredrik Mayor in his *American Ideas in Education* has summed up the contribution of John Dewey in these words, "In Dewey the voice of the pioneer, the stirring energies of the reformer, the patient method of the scientist and the faith of the teacher are united in a search for a new education through which man can survive in a chaotic age."

According to *Rusk*, "In education we cannot but be grateful to Dewey for his great services in challenging the old 'static cold storage ideal of knowledge' and in bringing education more into accord with the activities of present day life."

Regarding the work of Dewey, Irwin Edman (Ed.) in *John Dewey: His Contribution to American Tradition* (1955) has observed, "The breakdown of the violation of school from society, of book learning from vital experience, of the individual from his environment – the extent to which schools and colleges have removed these separations is a measure of the direct impact of refreshing reconstruction of Dewey's thinking".

Prof. Ulich in *History of Educational Thought* has summed up the contribution of John Dewey in these words, "Dewey's work encourages an experimental and scientific attitude. It shows what men can achieve if they rely on their reason and courage instead of clinging to their prejudice".

8

Philosophical Thought in India and Its Contribution to Education

RICH PHILOSOPHICAL HERITAGE

Indian philosophers and seers from the earliest times have thought deeply on the known and unknown and left no aspect of material existence or spiritual projects left untouched. No wherein else in the world did the human mind go deeper into the relationship of soul ('*Atman*') and Supreme Soul, i.e., God '*Brahman*'. In this context, views of some great Western scholars are quoted here.

1. *Francois Marie Voltaire* (1694-1774): French philosopher and writer, "I am convinced that everything has come down to us from the banks of the Ganga – astronomy, astrology, metaphysics, etc. The Vedas are the most precious gift for which the West has been indebted to the East".

2. *FrederichVon Sehlegel* (1772-1829): German critic, philosopher and writer, "there is no language in the world, even Greek, which has the clarity and the philosophical precision of Sanskrit. India is not only the origin of everything, she is superior in everything, intellectually, religiously, politically and even the Greek heritage seems pale in comparison".

3. *Arthur Schopenhauer* (1788-1860): German philosopher and writer, "In the whole world there is no study so beneficial and so elevating as that of the Upanishads. It has been solace of my life, and it will be the solace of my death. They are the product of the highest wisdom.

4. *Ralph Waldo Emerson* (1803-1883): American author, philosopher and essayist, "I owe a magnificent day to the Bhagwad Gita".

5. *Henry David Thoreau* (1817-1962): American philosopher and writer: "I bathe my intellect in the stupendous and cosmogonal philosophy of the Bhagwad Gita in comparison with which our modern world and its literature seems pumy".

6. *Prof. Max Mueller* (1823-1900): German philologist and philosopher, "In the history of the world, the Vedas fill a gap which no literary work in any language would fill. I maintain that to everybody who cares for himself for the ancestors, for his intellectual development, a study of the Vedic literature is indispensable. The Vedic literature opens to us a chapter what has been called the education of the human race, to which we can find no parallel anywhere else".

7. *Mark Twain* (1835-1910): American writer, "India is a land of religions, cradle of human race, birth place of human speech, grandmother of legend, greater grandmother of tradition".

8. *Alfred Northwhitehead* (1861-1947): British scholar, "The vastness of knowledge of today cannot transcend the *Buddhi* of the *Rishis* in ancient India, and science, in its most advanced stage now, is closer to Vedanta than ever before".

9. *Ella Wheeler Wilcox* (1850-1919): American poet and journalist, "In India, the land of Vedas, the remarkable works contain not only religious ideas for a perfect life but also facts which science has proved true. Electricity, radium, electronics, airship—all are known to the seers who founded the Vedas".

10. *George Bernard Shaw* (1856-1950): English dramatist, Nobel Laureate in literature, "The Indian way of life provides the vision of the natural way of life. We western veil ourselves with unnatural masks. On the face of India are the tender expressions which carry the marks of the creator's hand. This marks Hinduism the most tolerant religion of the world, because its one transcendent God includes all possible Gods".

11. *William Butler Yeats* (1856-1939): Irish dramatist, essayist, poet and Nobel Laureate. "It was my only first meeting with

the Indian philosophy that confirmed my vague speculations and seemed at once logical and boundless".

12. *H.G. Wells* (1866-1946): English author, historian and political philosopher, "There is space in its philosophy for everyone, which is one reason why India is a home to every single region of the world. Hinduism is synonymous with humanism. This is the essence in its great liberating quality".

13. *Herman Hesse* (1877-1962): German poet and novelist, noble laureate, "The marvel of the '*Bhagwad Gita*' in the truly beautiful revelation of life's wisdom which enables philosophy to blossom into religion".

14. *Romain Roland* (1894-1963): French Nobel Laureate and historian, "Religious faith in the case of the Hindus has never been allowed to run counter to scientific laws. Such tolerance may be surprising to religious believers in the West, but it is an integral part of Vedantic belief".

CHIEF SOURCES OF INDIAN PHILOSOPHICAL THOUGHT

The following are the chief sources from which Indian philosophical thought derives its inspiration:

1. Four Vedas
2. Six Vedangas
3. Four Upvedas
4. Four Brahamanas
5. One hundred and eight Upanishads (11 are most important)
6. Six systems of philosophy
7. The Bhagwad Gita
8. Three Smritis.

THE VEDIC PHILOSOPHICAL THOUGHT

Four Vedas: The four Vedas are the original and main sources of Vedic philosophy. Subsequent philosophies are based on the analysis and interpretation of the Vedas.

With a view to understand the philosophy of the Vedas, it is very necessary to understand the meaning of the word 'Veda'. Veda is derived from the root of Sanskrit word '*Vid*'. *Vid* means:

1. to know
2. to be
3. to obtain
4. to consider
5. to feel
6. to tell
7. to dwell

Thus the Vedas are concerned with:

1. Knowing God, Soul, Mind and Nature
2. To be one with God
3. To obtain salvation from the cycle of births and deaths
4. To consider various relationships—God and man, Man and nature, etc.
5. To feel oneness with God
6. To tell the glories of God
7. To dwell into the mysteries of universe and all existence

One and the Only One God

According to *Rig Veda* (1.164.46), God is one but the wise call Him by various names. Again *Yajurveda* (2.3.1) says, "He is addressed as Indra, Varuna and Agni". *Atharva Veda* states, "God is one and only one of His kind. He is called neither the second nor the third nor the fourth. He is called neither the fifth, nor the sixth nor yet the seventh. He is called neither the eighth, nor the ninth, nor yet the tenth. He takes care of all those who breathe or who do not breathe". *Rig Veda* (6.45.16) emphasises "One God alone is to be worshipped".

The Vedas declare God to be the essence of joy and bliss and that essence is in every object. All that exists is the abode of God. He is the indwelling spirit of the world. Let us wish for a life of one hundred years, full of activity. To be active is the only way to live well. All we do and have belongs to Him. Those who do not believe in the spiritual basis of life are 'soul killers'. They ruin their future and go to the regions of darkness. Man's mind is powerful, but it is nothing as compared to the universal Soul which pervades and permeates all. When man realises himself in all and in himself, he is free from the trials and tribulations of ignorance, and enjoys peace and bliss.

Threefold Areas of Contents of the Vedas

The contents of the Vedic philosophy may be categorised under the following three heads:

1. The '*Gyan*' or knowledge or wisdom
2. The '*Karma*' or action or code of conduct
3. The '*Upasana*' or dedication and devotion to God

Main Characteristics of the Thought of the Vedas

1. God is one and only one. He is all pervading, Omniscient, Omnipotent and ever present. He is the Supreme Spirit.
2. There are three entities in this universe—God, Soul and Matter.
3. The universe is real. It is not an illusion or dream.
4. This universe is created by God.
5. The soul is immortal.
6. The ultimate aim of life is to obtain salvation (*moksha*) and union with God.
7. Actions are followed by results—the 'Law of *Karma*'. The law of *Karma* is nothing else but the cause and its effect.
8. The theory of 'rebirth' is a necessary corollary of the Law of *Karma* and immortality of the soul.
9. Knowledge of truth should be acquired and dissipated.
10. Justice should be done to all creatures.
11. All human beings should live in peace and harmony.

The Vedas deal with every branch of knowledge and provide the basic knowledge of humanities, social sciences and natural and physical sciences. They deal with every aspect of human life—birth, childhood, youth, old age, death and rebirth. They point out the duties of a learned man, a student, a soldier, a householder, a warrior and an administrator etc. The Vedas have a message for all people of all nations and of all times. They embody the ways of leading a peaceful life.

The Vedas delve deep into the self as well as into the mysteries of God and nature to make life worth living. They are believed to be of divine origin.

The Vedas contain 20,358 verses: *Rig Veda* (10,522); *Atharva Veda* (5,977); *Yajur Veda* (1,984) and *Sama Veda* (1,875).

EDUCATIONAL IMPLICATIONS OF THE VEDIC THOUGHT

1. *Two Types of Education*: The Vedas mention two types of education, namely, '*paravidya*' and '*aparavidya*'. The former relates to spiritual or ecclesiastical knowledge and the latter relating to temporal or worldly matters. Both the types of education are needed.

2. *Objectives of Education*: Knowledge or learning makes one humble, free of ego. (A.V. VI. 41). Education must give due regard to the application of learning. (Y.V. XX. 12) O Lord! Illuminate the learner for a higher and happier life. (A.V. VII. 6.1).

According to R.K. Mukerjee, "Learning in India through the ages had been prized and pursued not for its own sake. It was sought as the means of salvation (*Moksha*) or self-realisation".

3. *Conducive Environment*: According to the Vedic view, through education one creates an environment conducive to attaining accomplishment of mind, intellect of thought, of purpose, of intelligence, of sense and vision. The parents, therefore, must have a selective environment.

4. *Significance of Women Education*: The Vedas give a very honourable and respectable status to women. They were eligible for higher education also. It is of interest to note that as many as 15 women scholars and seers contributed to several verses in the Vedas. Their names are: Angirasi, Shashwati, Apala, Indrani, Lopamudra, Guhu, Romsha, Sarama, Shraddha, Surya, Urvashi, Vagambhrani, Vasukra Patni, Visvasara and Yami. It is stated,

"O Learned Lady! All life is dependent on you, because you impart education to all". (R.V. II 97.17)

The Vedas accord a high position to the status of women and accordingly their education must receive priority.

5. *Education for World Peace and International Understanding*: The Vedas speak of one world and peace all around. Ideas and values of international understanding find their inspirations from the Vedas.

6. *Methods of Instruction*: These were as under:

(i) Lecture method
(ii) Meditation
(iii) Memorisation
(iv) Correct pronunciation
(v) Debates and discussions

7. *Organisation*: There was no state control on education.

8. *Teacher-pupil relations*: These were very close. The students were very respectful to the teachers who regarded them as their own children.

9. *Residential*: The teacher's home was the educational institution.

PHILOSOPHIC THOUGHT AS CONTAINED IN THE UPANISHADS

Major Source of All Indian Philosophical Thought: Different branches of Indian philosophies have been greatly influenced by Upanishads.

In the words of Schopenhaer (1788-1860), a German philosopher, "In the whole world there is no study so beneficial and elevating as that of the Upanishads. It has been the solace of life".

Prof. Max Mueller (1823-1900), another German philosopher endorses these views as, "If these words of Schopenhaer require endorsement, I shall willingly give it as the result of my own experience".

The *Upanishads* are the works of saints and seers. They deal with matter, soul and their relationships. They also point out how to lead a noble life.

Meaning of Upanishad: The word Upanishad consists of Sanskrit word '*Upa*' meaning 'nearby' and '*ni*' meaning 'sitting'. It, therefore, implies the 'sitting' of a disciple (student) in a devoted manner 'near' his spiritual 'Guru' (teacher or preceptor). Thus the term Upanishad means the knowledge received by the student 'sitting' close to the teacher.

Number of Upanishads: Traditionally, the number of Upanishads is given as 108. However, according to the great seer and scholar Swami Sankaracharya (788-820 A.D.), the principal Upanishads are 10 in number: 1. Isha, 2. Kenya, 3. Katha, 4. Prashna, 5. Mundaka, 6. Mandakya, 7. Chandogya, 8. Brihadaranyaka, 9. Aitareya, 10. Taitreya.

Period of Upanishads: Scholars are divided on the date of the composition of the Upanishads. Many of them, however, agree that most of the principal Upanishads belong to the period 7th century B.C.

Subjects Dealt with in the Upanishads: The Upanishads deal with knowledge (*Vidya*) which nullifies or destroys ignorance (*Avidya*) and takes the seeker to salvation (*Moksha*) and to Brahma (God) and help him to understand Him in the true sense and thus liberates him from the bondage of the world. (Freedom from the cycle of births and deaths).

The *Isha Upanishad* embodies in its very opening verse the central theme of all the Upanishads, namely, the spiritual unity and solidarity of all existence.

The second verse of the *Isha Upanishad* states that life is action. "In this world, one should desire to live one hundred years but only by performing actions".

Essence of the Upanishadic Thought

The essence of the Upanishadic thought may be summed up as under:

1. *Main Objective of Life*
   "From the Unreal lead me to the Real;
   From the Darkness lead me to the Light;
   From the Death lead me to Immortality".
   (*Brihadaranyaka*)
2. *Realisation of the Supreme*: Supreme is realised by truth, austerity, proper knowledge and self-control. (*Mundaka*)
3. *Passion for Truth*: The mental climate as illustrated in the Upanishads is saturated with a passion for truth and a similar passion for human happiness and welfare.
4. *Knowledge*: Knowledge gained through one-pointed determination removes, shatters or destroys avidya (ignorance or spiritual blindness).
5. *Rightful living*: "Do not covet the wealth of anyone". (*Isha*)
6. *Wise man*: "The wise man who realises all beings as not distinct from his own self, does not by virtue of that perception, hate anyone". (*Isha*)
7. *Life is Action*: "In this world, one should desire to live one hundred years, but only by performing actions". (*Isha*)
8. *Constant Effort*: "Arise, awake and stop not till the goal is reached". (*Katha*)
9. *Freedom*: Physical freedom, mental freedom and the spiritual freedom are the watch words of the Upanishads.
10 *Universal Man*: The Upanishads stand in the forefront in proclaiming the concept of 'Universal Man'.

Educational Implications of the Upanishadic Approach

1. *Aims of Education*: The principal aims of education according to Upanishads are:

(i) Self-realisation or spiritual development.
(ii) Acquisition of supreme knowledge.
(iii) Character development.
(iv) Cultural development.
(v) Development of social virtues.

2. *Questioning Approach*: Of the 10 principal Upanishads, the *Prashna*, as its name implies, is an Upanishad of questions. Each of the 6 chapters comprises a question asked by each of a group of 6 inquiring students and the answers given by the teacher.

3. *Most Intimate Teacher-Pupil Relationship*: Education involving the student 'sitting close (near) to' the teacher means the most intimate student-teacher communion.

4. *Earnestness*: The earnestness of the search for truth is one of the important features of the Upanishads.

5. *Inquiring Mind*: The seeker must have an inquiring mind (*Jigyasa*) and the teacher must satisfy the inquiring mind.

6. *Moral Training*: According to the Upanishads, a rigorous moral training is the necessary prelude to spiritual knowledge.

7. *Significant Place of the Teacher in the Upanishadic Approach to Education and Learning*: The Upanishadic approach assigns an important place to the teacher as the communicator of knowledge and wisdom. According to the Upanishadic approach, the truth is not to be comprehended by the mere logical process of argumentation and dialectics. Only the great teacher could impart the Supreme Knowledge. The Katha Upanishad says, "He (the self) of whom many are not even able to hear, whom many even when they hear of him, do not comprehend, wonderful is a man, who found, who is able to teach him (the self), wonderful is he who comprehends him, when taught by an able teacher".

The teacher was expected to possess virtues of affection, humility and truthfulness etc. Plain living, high thinking, disciplined routine, abstinence from pleasures, mental control and above all sincerity were the chief characteristics of an ideal teacher. The Brahmachari or the student was under the direct observation of his teacher all twenty-four hours and was also expected to lead a pious and disciplined life.

8. *Methods of Study*: Listening, practice or recitation, immediate apprehension of the meaning, discourses and disputation were the methods generally followed.

PHILOSOPHICAL THOUGHT OF THE *BHAGWAD GITA*

A Unique Book: *Srimadbhagwad Gita* is considered by several scholars as the epitome of Indian thought.

Sri Aurobindo, the revolutionary turned philosopher and sage has stated the importance of *Gita* in these words "All we need of spiritual truth for the spiritual life is to be found in the *Gita.*"

Sri Swami Parmananda describes the essence of *Bhagwad Gita* as "From the simple duty task to the most exhalted state of spiritual consciousness at every step of the soul's evolution, one may turn to this sacred book for inspiration. The *Bhagwad Gita* stands as a summary of all scriptures teaching the essence of the Vedas."

The *Gita* is so popular that it has more than 50 commentaries in Sanskrit and more than 250 commentaries in other Indian and foreign languages. Almost every year we find a new book on the meaning and message of Gita. It is ascribed to seer Veda Vyasa.

In size, the *Gita* is a little book of seven hundred verses. The verses are divided into eighteen chapters. It is in the form of a dialogue between Arjuna, a noted commander and Shri Krishna, an earthly manifestation of God—'*Avatara*'. The setting of the dialogue is highly dramatic. Arjuna is facing the huge army of his cousins with their supporters, many of whom are his elders including his '*guru*' Dronacharya. Arjuna is to strike them for the enforcement of their claim (Five Pandavas) to the part of the ancestral kingdom which is not accepted by Duryodhana, leader of the Kauravas. The sight of his dear ones dissolves his determination to fight and he lays down his arms and thinks of renouncing the world. Shri Krishna, who is acting as his charioteer urges him to fight for his right cause. Krishna succeeds in persuading Arjuna who ultimately wins the struggle.

The wonderful dialogue closes on the note of dedicated activity, promising glory, success and prosperity to the individual who combines physical valour, with divine wisdom and is entitled Moksha or communication with God through liberating dedication.

Principal Teaching of Gita

1. *Immortality of Soul*: The soul is immortal and the body is perishable. The cycle of creation is a hard fact from which there is no escape.

2. *Theory of Incarnations* (*avatars*): The ordered progress of the world at large is so important that God takes on special forms of prophets of incarnations from time to time to ensure its progress by appropriate guidance.

3. *Doing Duty as Dharma*: The essence of the philosophy as contained in the Gita is with inner convictions. We should discharge our duties diligently and honestly irrespective of the consequences and leave the rest to the Almighty. We must fight for justice and the right cause.

4. *Death is Certain*. Death is inevitable to one who is born. One who dies, is bound to take birth. It does not, therefore, behove one to grieve over an inevitable event.

5. *Action or Karma Yoga*: The whole theme of the third chapter is the philosophy of action. This is also known as '*Karma-Yoga*' - communication with God through action.

6. *Two Ways of Liberation*: According to Gita, there are two ways of liberation—those of action and knowledge. However, the order of activity is more important. It combines personal good with social good.

7. *Social Welfare*: To be content with personal perfection is a narrow ideal. The proper ideal is to give to the world the best and the most that one can and to take from it the least. The wise man acts as a source of guidance and inspiration to the ignorant masses.

8. *Attainment of Moksha* (*Liberation*): The wonderful dialogue closes on the note of dedicated activity promising glory, success and prosperity to the individual who combines physical valour, with divine wisdom and is entitled Moksha or communication with God through liberating dedication. One can be united with Him if one transforms one's action into Him. This is real renunciation.

Selected Verses from *Bhagwad* Gita

Soul is Immortal

As the indweller in the body experiences childhood, youth and old age in the body, he also passes on to another body. The serene one is not affected thereby. (*Adhaya* 2.13)

The soul is neither born nor does it die. Coming into being and ceasing to be do not take place in it. Unborn, eternal, constant and ancient, it is not killed when the body is slain. (*Adhaya* 2.20)

As a man, casting off worn-out garments puts on new ones, so the soul, casting off worn-out bodies enters into the other that is new. (*Adhaya* 2.22)

Weapons do not cleave the soul, fire burns it not, water wets it not, wind dries it not. (*Adhaya* 2.23)

Death is Certain

Death is certain of that which is born, birth is certain of that which is dead. You should not lament over the inevitable. (*Adhaya* 2.27)

Action! Action! Action!

Seek to perform your duty; but lay not claim to its fruits. Be you not the producer of the fruits of *Karma*; neither shall you lean towards inaction. (*Adhaya* 2.47)

Perform action, O Dhanajaya, being fixed in yoga, renouncing attachments and even-minded in success and failure; equilibrium is verily yoga. (*Adhaya* 2.48)

Concentration of Mind

When also, like a tortoise its limbs, he can withdraw the senses from sense objects, his wisdom is then set firm. (*Adhaya* 2.57)

The excited senses, O son of Kunti, impetuously carried away the mind of even a wise man, striving for perfection. (*Adhaya* 2.60)

From anger proceeds delusion; from delusion, confused memory; from confused memory the ruin of reason; due to the ruin of reason, an individual perishes. (*Adhaya* 2.63)

Just as a gale pushes away a ship on the water, the mind that yields to the roving senses, carries away his discrimination. (*Adhaya* 2.67)

EDUCATIONAL IMPLICATIONS OF PHILOSOPHIC THOUGHT OF GITA

The greatest lesson for the learner is that he must have complete faith in his teacher who should also be devoted to his work. True knowledge, learning and wisdom are acquired through ceaseless action coupled with devotion. Concentration on studies leads to enlightenment and self-control. The main characteristics of the learner or a devotee are: He is a lover of knowledge and mankind. He is curious to know and has an abiding faith in his teacher. He very politely but with a subtle resolution puts questions to his teacher to solve his problems. The teacher also makes all possible efforts to enlighten his students and guides him in such a way as he attains the ideals of a self-realised individual.

Following are in brief the main implications of the teachings of Gita:

1. Development of virtuous knowledge.
2. Coordination between the individual and social aim.
3. Development of inner consciousness.
4. Establishing the importance of duty in life.
5. Development of logical and intellectual ability.
6. Close spiritual relation between the teacher and the taught.
7. Pursuit of ideas with single minded devotion.

(*See also* Buddhism and Jainism, Swami Vivekananda, Sri Aurobindo, Tagore and Gandhiji, Constitutional Provisions, Composite Culture of India).

SYSTEMS OF PHILOSOPHY AND THEIR EDUCATIONAL IMPLICATIONS

India has a very rich tradition of philosophical thought. In ancient India, six systems of philosophy emerged as a result of contemplation of six seers.

Chart Showing Six Systems of Philosophy and Their Propounders

(1)	(2)	(3)	(4)	(5)	(6)
Samkhya	*Vaisesika*	*Nyay*	*Yoga*	*Mimamsa*	*Vedanta*
(Kapila)	(Kanada)	(Gautama)	(Patanjali)	(Jamimini)	(Badarayana) Shankara or Sankara of the 8th Century is considered as the greatest exponent of this thought

According to some thinkers, Buddhism and Jainism are the other two in this category.

Vaisesika System of Philosophy

This system of philosophy founded by Sage Kanada attempts to distinguish between the various kinds of ultimate objects and to classify all these under the following five elements:

(i) Earth ('*Prithvi*')
(ii) Water ('*Jal*')
(iii) Air ('*Vayu*')
(iv) Fire ('*Agni*')
(v) Ether ('*Akash*')

These elements exist in the form of Atom, Time, Space, Mind and Self. The creation of the world begins when the atoms of these five elements start to combine. When these elements disintegrate, the world comes to an end.

Salvation, according to Vaisesika depends on when one fully recognises the atomic nature of the universe and its difference with the soul.

Vaisesika seeks to explain the world by reference to original diversity and comes to establish rather a rough view of self and God. It has very little practical value.

Nyaya System of Philosophy

Important features of the Nyaya system of philosophy are:

1. It considers God as the creator of the world.
2. It is a science of reasoning.
3. It makes a detailed study of the sources or testimonies of knowledge (*pramana*).
4. For arriving at some conclusion, it considers the following aspects:
   (i) Perception (*Pratyaksha*)
   (ii) Inference (*Anumana*)
   (iii) Comparison (*Upamana*)
   (iv) Verbal, i.e., words (*Sabda*)

Sankhya System of Philosophy

The Sankhya philosophy is founded by the Sage Kapila who is said to have flourished about the seventh century B.C. It is the oldest philosophy.

According to this philosophy, soul is immortal. The '*Atman*' (soul) pervades all and is indestructible. Only the physical bodies end. The pure soul neither kills nor is killed. Bodies are like garments to be cast off when old and replaced by fresh ones. With the changing states, bodies appear and disappear.

Birth, childhood, youth, old age and death are the various modes of the soul, which owns or casts off the body.

Body's contact with the physical elements brings about pain and pleasure, which should be endured as the sensations are passing phases.

We must keep our body in a state of strength and vigour so as to live well and to discharge our obligations in a satisfying way to ourselves and to society.

Sankhya identifies three principles or qualities ('*Gunas*' in the formation of personalities—*Satva* or goodness, *Rajas* or passion and *Tamas* or darkness. A well-balanced personality is based on the principal of 'Satva'—good contemplation, good thoughts, good understanding and good (pure) food.

The three characteristics are sometimes illustrated as given in the chart.

An ideal personality has *Satva* traits in all his actions.

There is another interpretation of *Sankhya* philosophy. According to this philosophy, there are twenty-five basic principles (*Tatvas*). Of these first is *Prakriti*, i.e. *matter*. It is from matter that all elements like air, water, weather (*akasa*), intelligence (*buddhi*), self-consciousness, sight, touch, hearing, etc. develop. One of the most important *tatvas* is *Purusa* (soul). *Purusa* is not dependent upon *Prakriti*. Likewise *Prakriti* is dependent on *Purusa*. Salvation lies in understanding this difference.

Three Characteristics of Sankhya Doctrine

'*Satva*' trait implies	'*Rajas*' signifies	'*Tamas*' means
(i) Truth	(i) Fierceness	(i) Darkness
(ii) Wisdom	(ii) Violence	(ii) Gloomy
(iii) Goodness	(iii) Passion	(iii) Foolishness
(iv) Beauty		(iv) Undesirable traits

Yoga

Meaning of Yoga: According to sage Patanjali, the author of an ancient book '*Yoga Sastra*' (circa second B.C.), Yoga is a method of controlling the tendencies of mind. Some scholars regard yoga as an attempt of uniting oneself with the Supreme Spirit, i.e. *Paramatma* or God. Yoga is also described as a way of life for the harmonious development of the body, mind and soul. What Yoga is Not! Very often, Yoga is misunderstood and thought of in terms of certain exercises or *asanas* (postures) for training the body. This is a very narrow concept or meaning of Yoga. It is certainly not a physical act or exercise only. It is much more.

Nature of Yoga: The aim of Yoga is to control one's desires and aspirations. Yoga strives to understand the real nature of soul. This can be best understood by controlling one's desires and aspirations. The state of Yoga can be achieved only by controlling one's desires and lusts. Just as we cannot see the true image of a thing in disturbed water, when the mind is unstable and out of control, we cannot perceive God. Yoga meditation is necessary to get a glimpse of God.

Components of Yoga: Yoga has eight components called *Ashtanga*. These are—*Yama, Niyama, Asana, Pranayama, Pratyahara, Dharana, Dhyana* and *Samadhi*. By following these components ignorance is removed and real knowledge is achieved. As the follower (*Sadhak*) proceeds higher and higher, his ignorance is removed and his wisdom is awakened. So the main aim of Yoga is to remove ignorance and to achieve wisdom.

Stages or Branches of Yoga

According to sage Patanjali, following are the eight stages of Yoga:

1. *Yama* (*Self-control*): This refers to the moral discipline for the individual and it includes truth, the practice of *brahmacharya* (celibacy), non-stealing, non-receiving of gifts and observance of the creed of non-violence.

2. *Niyama* (*Observance*): It means self-purification by practising austerity, purity, contentment, studying scriptures and surrendering oneself to God.

3. *Asanas* (*Postures*): This implies practising certain body-postures for acquiring health and developing steadfastness of mind. *Asanas* (exercises or postures) have been developed over the centuries and they help in exercising every muscle, nerve and gland of the body.

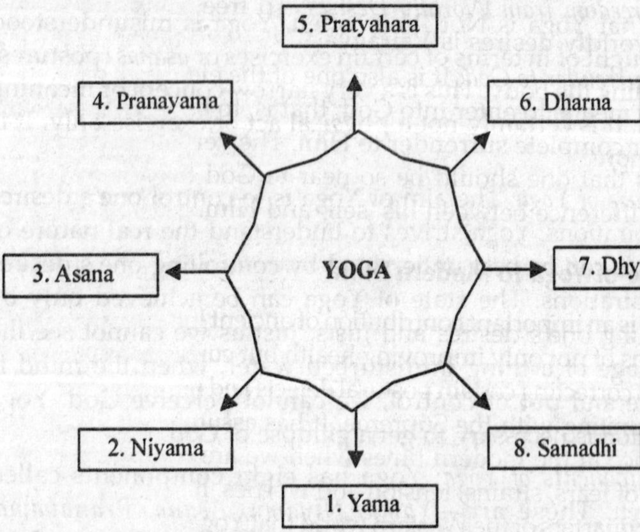

Fig. 8.1: Components of Yoga

4. *Pranayama (Control of Breath)*: It is the practice of controlling breath for strengthening the respiratory system, purifying blood and soothing the mind.

5. *Pratyahara (Restraint)*: This is an attempt to free the mind from the domination or control of senses.

6. *Dharana (Steadying the Mind)*: This is concentration on a single object or point.

7. *Dhyana*: It refers to the concentration on the all-pervading divinity through practice.

8. *Samadhi (Meditation)*: This is the last stage of Yoga. In this stage, the yogi merges himself with the Divine Spirit, although he is alert and conscious.

Controlling Factors of Mental Processes

Exercise, freedom from worldly desires, and surrender to God are the three main means of control:

(i) *Exercise*: Exercise is necessary to make any state or situation stable. When exercise is continuous and is done with devotion, it becomes fixed strongly.

(ii) *Freedom from Worldly Desires*: To free the mind from worldly desires is Vairagya.

(iii) *Surrender to God*: It is also one of the elements of Yoga. It means to enter into God, that is, to be one with Him or complete surrender to Him. The very aim of prayer is that one should be so near to God that there is no difference between his 'self' and Him.

Relevance of Yoga to Modern Mind

Yoga is an important contribution of ancient India to the world as a means of not only improving health but curing some mental maladies, correcting certain postural defects and removing tension but also uniting with the Supreme. It has assumed all the more significance in the modern times when we are confronted with all kinds of fears, strains, tension and worries. It is now believed in certain quarters of the Western world that Yoga can solve man's several problems and bring peace of mind.

Mimamsa

Sage Jaimini is the originator of this system. It dates back to the fourth century B.C. Jaimini's *Sutras* number two thousand and five hundred. Jaimini stated that due performance of duty as laid down in the Vedas should lead to heaven where there are eternal joys and pleasures. He had an abounding faith in man and his efforts. He laid down ethical purity as the qualifying condition for the performance of the Vedic rituals.

He also enunciated the law of action, holding that every act generates a potency, which comes to surface in its own time.

He propounded *Karma* (Action) as the *Dharma* (Duty). Thus according to him work is the essential duty of man.

This system recognises three paths of salvation. One is concerned with the *Karma Kanda* (ritualism) in accordance with the Vedas. Second is concerned with the *jnanakanda* (pursuit of knowledge) of the Vedas. The third is concerned with the performance of duties in accordance with the teachings of the Vedas.

Vedanta

The literal meaning is end (*anta*) of the Vedas. In this sense, the term is used for the Upanishads. In addition, the Vedanta is one of the six systems of philosophy. According to this school, the highest wisdom of the Vedas is to be found in the Upanishads. Its essence is contained in the phrase '*Tat Twam Asi*' or "That Thou Art". 'That' refers to the Supreme One or *Brahman* and 'Thou', refers to the individual soul or '*Atman*'.

Thus the ultimate goal of life is the realisation of the truth that only Brahman or the Supreme One is real. The material world is '*maya*' or illusion. Spiritual knowledge alone is '*Brahmavidya*'. This knowledge is a means of salvation.

The union of the soul and *Brahma* is salvation. Just as the river loses its identity after falling into the ocean, soul loses its identity after being united with the *Brahman*.

Educational Implications of the Six Systems of Philosophy

All the six systems, by and large, stress the elements of reasoning and critical thinking. There is a great need to emphasise the eight elements of yoga in our educational institutions. It may be noted that 'yoga' is not merely for physical fitness but more importantly for the all-round upliftment of the individual. It should be accepted as a way of life. It develops mental faculty, relieves tension and provides peace of mind and inner solace.

SALIENT FEATURES OF INDIAN THOUGHT AND IMPLICATIONS

Four Pillars of Indian Thought

Indian thought determines the ideals and ways of life that we should adopt. It is focussed on the following four elements:

1. '*Dharma*'. Righteousness.
2. '*Artha*'. Necessities of life.
3. '*Kama*'. Satisfaction of our urges.
4. '*Moksha*'. Liberation.

Dharma (*Righteousness*): It is a spiritual value. '*Dharma*' is not only a central concept of Indian philosophy but also a unique one. It determines what we ought to do in different situations. In fact it regulates one's life. The word '*dharma*' comes from the Sanskrit root '*dhr*' meaning thereby 'to hold' or to 'sustain'. '*Dharma*' denotes right action or right conduct. It has ethical and social values. It includes virtues of control of senses, charity, honesty, love, non-injury, self-restraint, etc. '*Dharma*' puts a check on selfishness. '*Adharma*' is vice.

According to the social concept of ancient Indian thought of '*Dharma*', the ideal life consists of four '*Ashramas*' (stages): '*Brahmacharya*', the period of education and period of celibacy, '*Grihasthya*', the life of the householder, '*Vanaprasthya*', retreat from worldly bonds and finally '*Sanyasa*', the life of a hermit.

Artha: (Wealth or material things). This is only helpful as a means of satisfying one or the other desire of human life.

Kama: Includes physical as well as the psychological satisfaction of the natural urges of a person. Wealth or money is valuable only to the extent it serves, as a means to acquire goods. '*Artha*' thus is an instrument value and it is a means to the realisation of '*Kama*'.

'*Artha*' and '*Kama*' are sought not only by man but also by all living beings.

Moksha (Liberation or salvation). This concept sums up the aim of life in Indian philosophy. It is the realisation of the self. It is spiritual bliss. It is freedom from the cycle of births and deaths. It is becoming 'one' with God. It is the highest attainment man can have. It is the loftiest end. Philosophers and seers have prescribed different ways for the realisation of '*moksha*'. Two of these are most important. One prescribes the practice of '*niskam karma*' (selfless action), leading a pure life. The second prescribes '*dhyana*' (meditation).

A household is expected to earn ('*Artha*') through right ways and spend it rightly for the satisfaction of his needs ('*Kama*') so that he attains '*Moksha*'.

According to some thinkers '*Moksha*' can be realised after

death while others think that it can be realised in this very life. In any case the emphasis is on purity and noble deeds.

Is Indian Thought Individualistic? Certainly Not

There are critics who criticise Indian thought as they consider it to be totally individualistic. They sometimes charge that Indian thought disregards social values and is negative and passive. They sum up the Indian thought as making people totally unworldly. According to them it teaches one to become '*Sanyasi*'. They think that '*Dharma*' means individual perfection and running away from the daily pursuits.

While discussing Indian thought it must be stressed that the idealist in India, while talking of the infinite goal does not neglect the immediate objectives of life. Self-realisation or salvation is to be realised in the society. The Indian philosophers very clearly, prescribed four stages of life. Each stage involved certain duties. They believed that the performance of these duties would lead to liberation. Accordingly these duties and values were reflected in the curriculum. Education was considered a means of attaining salvation. Knowledge and wisdom were not gained for their sake but to make man moral and thereby assist him in realising the ultimate objective of life.

Swami Vivekananda, one of the greatest exponents of Indian philosophy observed, "So long as millions live in hunger and ignorance, I hold every man a traitor who, having been educated at their expense, pays not the least heed to them, I call him a '*mahatma*' who feels for the poor. Let these people be your God-think of them, work for them."

Two Paths of Salvation

The Indian way of life or Indian philosophy propounds two paths for self-realisation: *Pravrtimarga* (the path of active life) and *niviritimarga* (the path of renunciation). The main concern of Indian philosophy is *sarvajana sukhino bhavantu* (happiness for all mankind). What is recommended is not 'renunciation of the world but 'self-renunciation'. Unselfishness or 'selfless' is the central point of Indian philosophy.

The *Gayatri Mantra* embodies the essence of Indian thought.

Aum Bhur Bhuvah Svah
Tat Savitur Varenyam
Bhargo Devasya Dhimahi
Dhiyo Yoh Nah Prachodayat

Aum, the celestial sound that resounds in our bodies,
Over the earth and the cosmos up to the gates of heaven,
The effulgence of the rising sun that sets all living things,
To their allotted tasks to strive to achieve their aims in life,
May the dazzling light which is the gift of the gods,
Illuminate our beings,
Let us contemplate on it,
So that our minds gain enlightenment.

Main Elements of Indian Thought

These may be summarised as under:

1. Following the path of truth.
2. Wishing happiness and welfare of the entire humanity.
3. Treating all human beings as friends.
4. Doing one's duty honestly.
5. Eschewing pride.
6. Showing respects to all faiths.
7. Having faith in the freedom of worship.
8. Realising self-being one with the Divine—attaining *Moksha* (Liberation).
9. Earning through righteous means.
10. Following a life of purity and enjoying the pleasures of life according to *Dharma*.
11. Following the spiritual path for salvation.
12. Attaining highest knowledge and wisdom.

Educational Implications of Indian Philosophical Thought

Two Types of Education: The Vedas mention two types of education, namely, *paravidya* and *aparavidya*. The former relates to spiritual or ecclesiastical knowledge and the latter relating to temporal or worldly matters. The intellectual development, moral development and vocational development are the broad aims of education and curriculum should include contents and activities accordingly.

Suitable Environment: According to the Indian thought, through education one creates environment conducive to attain accomplishment of mind, intellect of thought, of purpose, of intelligence, of sense and vision. Education begins in the mother's womb. Preparation has to be made to make the womb a fit receptacle for a worthy promising soul. The mind of the pregnant mother and the environment she is in, have a shaping influence on the child who is yet to be born. The parents, therefore, must have selective environment.

Indian thought stresses close contact between the teacher and the taught for the development of character and personality. Residential educational institutions should be established wherever possible.

Methods of Teaching-Learning: Lectures, meditation, concentration, questions-answers, discussions and debates are the important methods of instruction and learning.

Education of Women: The Vedas accord a high position to the status of women and accordingly their education must receive priority. It would be of interest to note that nearly 20 women seers and scholars are mentioned in the Rig Veda who composed Vedic hymns.

Value Education: The essence of Indian thought is contained in leading a pure and noble life. It is founded on value education and at present is an urgent need to provide value education primarily through personal examples of the elders and value related practical activities.

Free from State Interference: There should be no state interference in the functioning of educational institutions.

9

Swami Vivekananda's Philosophy and its Impact on Education

BRIEF LIFE SKETCH OF SWAMI VIVEKANANDA

Early Life. Vivekananda's original name was Narendranath Dutt. He acquired the new name in 1886 when he took *Sanyasa.*

He was born in Calcutta in 1863. His father was a practicing lawyer at Calcutta High Court. Under the influence of his mother he made a deep study of Hindu scriptures. At college he was adept in boxing, riding, swimming and wrestling. He was an ardent student of philosophy and poetry. He graduated with honours from Calcutta University.

Education. He had an excellent command over Bengali, English and Sanskrit. He was a voracious reader and had a sharp memory. He could often display a verbatim familiarity with the *Encyclopaedia Britannica.* His principal Rev. W.W. Hastie once remarked, "Narendranath is really a genius. I have travelled far and wide but I have never yet come across a lad of his talents and possibilities, even in German Universities, among philosophical students".

Meeting with Shri Ramakrishna—A Turning Point in Life

He was deeply interested in the study of philosophy and religion. For sometime he was a classroom teacher also. His search for truth led him to Ramakrishna Paramhansa, at Dakshineswar in 1882. Though not literate, Swami Ramakrishna was an enlightened soul. During the next six years of his association with the master, he had a spiritual transformation and emerged as Swami Vivekananda. He left home and travelled all over India. His wandering left him deeply affected by the despair and poverty of the masses of India.

Swami Vivekananda organised the Ramakrishna Mission in 1886, after the passing away of his master.

In 1888, 2 years after his master's death, he set out to the Himalayas. He wandered for 2 years through deserts and forests. In Kanyakumari, after worshipping in the temple, Vivekananda sat on a rock, and meditated for sometime. He went to America in 1893.

Soul-stirring Address at the World Parliament of Religions at Chicago (USA) in 1893. On September 11, 1893, on the opening day of the Parliament, he sat rapt in silent meditation. In the afternoon session he rose to speak. He bowed down to *Saraswati*, the Devi (goddess of learning) and addressed the audience as, "Sisters and brothers of America". Before he could utter another word, people were so much mesmerised that there was applause for full two minutes. When silence was restored, he began his address. His wisdom coupled with universal message of love and tolerance made him a world teacher. In his address, he said that upon the banner of every religion will soon be written, "HELP and not FIGHT', 'ASSIMILATION and not DESTRUCTION', 'HARMONY and PEACE and not DISSENSION'. The Parliament of Religion lasted seventeen days and Swamiji addressed six times.

Message of Spirituality and Social Service. He addressed several meetings in the USA, UK, Sri Lanka and spread the spiritual message.

Swami Vivekananda devoted the rest of his strenuous life in communicating his message of unity and tolerance.

In India, he organised social work also in addition to spiritual pursuits.

MAJOR PUBLICATIONS OF SWAMI VIVEKANANDA

1. *The Complete Works of Swami Vivekananda* – 9 Volumes.
2. *Bhaktiyoga.*

3. *Advaita Vedanta.*
4. *Education.*
5. *Jnana Yoga.*
6. *Lectures from Colombo to Almora.*
7. *Memories of European Travels.*
8. *Philosophical and Religious Lectures of Swami Vivekananda.*
9. *Swami Vivekananda at the Parliament of Religions.*

PRINCIPAL FEATURES OF SWAMI VIVEKANANDA'S PHILOSOPHY

1. God resides in every human heart.
2. The best worship of God is service to mankind.
3. Ethics and morality should be the real basis of life.
4. Love and renunciation should permeate the universe.
5. Religion means self-realisation through self-control.

SWAMI VIVEKANANDA'S PHILOSOPHY OF EDUCATION

Following are the main elements of the philosophy of Swami Vivekananda:

1. All knowledge is in the human mind.
2. Education is the manifestation of the perfection already in man.
3. Knowledge is inherent in man. No knowledge comes from outside.
4. Like fire in a piece of flint, knowledge exists in the mind. Man discovers it.
5. The infinite library of the universe is in our mind.

Swami Vivekananda explains this as, "We say Newton discovered gravitation. The falling of an apple gave the suggestion to Newton and then he studied his own mind. He rearranged all the previous links of thought in his mind and discovered a link among them, which we call the law of gravitation".

SWAMI VIVEKANANDA ON VARIOUS ASPECTS OF EDUCATION

I. Aim of Education: Man-Making

According to Swamiji, education is the manifestation of divinity already existing in man. Education is not the imparting of facts. "If education were identical with information, the libraries would be the greatest sages in the world and encyclopaedias the Rishis". He further observed, "Will you consider a man as educated if only he can pass some examinations and deliver good lectures? The education which does not help the common mass of people to equip themselves for the struggle for life, which does not bring out strength of character, a spirit of philanthropy, and the courage of a lion—is it worth the name?

Swami Vivekananda saw the 'Divine' in the form of the poor whom he called *Daridra Narayan*.

Swami Vivekananda saw the 'Divine' in the form of the poor whom he called *Daridra Narayan*. This denotes the direction of 'Man-making' education. It implies that education should develop a spirit of service and the poor and the needy must be helped to raise themselves.

Man-making education also brings out the significance of the famous words said by Vivekananda at the Parliament of Religions held in 1893 at Chicago. These were: HELP, ASSIMILATION, HARMONY and PEACE. Accordingly education should develop these qualities in man.

Man-making education is inherent in character development as well as vocational development. Man-making education is a very comprehensive concept.

Following are the chief elements of man-making concept for which education should be directed to:

1. Swami Vivekananda believed in the Vedanata philosophy which considers that the ultimate goal of human life is to attain 'Unity with the Creator'. An individual must fully understand this.

2. Service to man is equated with devotion to God. According to Swami Vivekananda, God resides in every human heart. Thus man should develop the spirit of service to his fellow beings.
3. Swami Vivekananda believed in the liberal concept of religion. Essential elements of all religions are the same. No religion is inferior to other religion. Man should follow an attitude of respect for all religions.
4. According to Vivekananda, love is the highest goal of religion. Man should imbibe love for all and hatred for none.
5. Swami Vivekananda developed a synthesis between science and spirituality. Man should attain knowledge of science and spirituality.
6. Swami Vivekananda was a prophet of humanity. His concept of man transcends the cultural boundaries of the East and the West. He was a rationalist and a man must develop rational attitude in life.

II. Role of the Teacher

Vivekananda laid stress on the following qualities that a teacher should have:

1. The first condition is that he should be sinless.
2. The second condition is that he should know the spirit of scriptures.
3. The third condition is the spiritual force of the teacher should be based on love for the students.
4. The fourth condition is that the teacher should think that he is only helping the child to grow. He is the external teacher and he offers the suggestion which arouses the internal teacher, i.e., the mind of the child.

III. Principles of Teaching-learning

Swami Vivekananda emphasised the following:

1. *Self-teaching*: "No one was ever taught by another. Each of us has to teach himself. A child educates itself."

2. *Living Examples of Teacher*: "Words even thoughts, contribute only one-third of the influence in making an impression—the man two-thirds."
3. *Teaching through Positive Suggestions*: "We should give positive ideas. Negative ideas only weaken men. If you speak kind words to them and encourage them, they are bound to improve in time."
4. *Concentration as the Only Method of Education*: "The power of concentration is the only key to the treasure-house of knowledge."
5. *Qualities of the Learner*: "The conditions necessary for the taught are purity, a real thirst after knowledge and perseverance."

IV. Physical and Health Education

"Be strong, my young friends... you will be nearer to Heaven through football than through the study of Gita".

V. Education to be Based on Western Science Coupled with *Vedanta*

"Living with the Guru and a similar system of imparting education are needed. What we want is Western science coupled with *Vedanta*—'*Brahmacharya*' as the guiding motto and also '*Shraddha*' (faith) in one's own self".

VI. Education of the Masses

Vivekananda gave prime importance to the education of the masses. He asserted, "The chief cause of India's ruin has been the monopolising of the whole education of the land, by dint of pride and royal authority, among a handful of men". He further observed, "If we are to rise again, we shall have to do it in the same way, that is, by spreading education among the masses". He considers that "The great national sin is the neglect of the masses, and that is one of the chief causes of our downfall. No amount of politics would be of any avail until the masses in India are once more well-educated, well-fed, and cared for. They pay for our education, they build our temples, but in return they get kicks. They are practically our slaves, if we want to regenerate India, we must work for them".

VII. Women's Education

Vivekananda was an ardent champion of the education of women. He remarked, "Women have many grave problems but none that cannot be solved by that magic word: education!"

VIII. Secular Education

Vivekananda had great regard for all religions. "Let us take in all that has been in the past, enjoy the light of the present and open every window of the heart for all that will come in the future. Salutation to all the prophets of the past, to all the great ones of the present and to all that are to come in the future."

CONTRIBUTION OF SWAMI VIVEKANANDA TO EDUCATION: RELEVANCE OF HIS VIEWS TODAY

1. He laid stress on the character development education.
2. He advocated the education of the masses which implies adult education and free and compulsory education regardless of caste, creed or colour. He said, "I consider that the greatest national sin is the neglect of the masses."
3. He revived the spirit of humanism in education.
4. His clarion call to the educated people was, "So long as the millions live in hunger and ignorance, I hold every man a traitor who, having been educated at their expense, pays not the least heed to them".
5. He considered the education of women as the chief instrument of national regeneration.

Summing up: Educational needs of modern India are reflected in the Preamble to our Constitution. It is clear that educational aims, contents and methods of teaching and in fact the entire process of education must be based on these pillars – Secularism, Socialism and Democracy. From the educational philosophy of Swami Vivekananda as stated above, it is clear that he visualised the needs of independent India and accordingly he set forth his philosophical thought. His views are quite relevant today. He was for a liberal approach to religion and accordingly advocated values of secularism. He believed that ignorance was the most important evil of the society. He advocated mass education, i.e., free and compulsory education as well as, adult education. His advocacy of women education is in accordance with the present day needs. His stress on child-centred education is another remarkable aspect of his educational philosophy. He advocated a system of education that was egalitarian.

Swami Vivekananda's views on education may be summed up in his own words, "We want that education by which character is formed, strength of mind is increased, the intellect is expanded and by which one stands on one's own feet".

10

Rabindranath Tagore (1869-1941): Educational Philosophy and its Impact

BRIEF LIFE SKETCH

Popularly called Gurudev, Rabindranath Tagore was born in a family known for its progressive views. He was born at Calcutta on May 6, 1861. He wrote his first verse in his eighth year. His schools days was not happy. He studied for sometime in England to become a barrister. Tagore conducted his educational experiments at Shantiniketan. He burst into fame when '*Gitanjali*' won him Nobel Prize for literature in 1913. He utilised the entire amount of award of $8000 for the upkeep of his school at Shantiniketan, which in due course became the Visvabharati University. Tagore visited Europe, Japan, Russia and United States.

Tagore was given the title of 'Knight' in 1915 but he was so pained and stirred by the Jallianwala Bagh Massacre, Amritsar in 1919 that he returned this title. At that time he wrote to the Viceroy of India, "The time has come when badges of honour make our shame, glaring in their incongruous context of humiliation, and I for my part wish to stand, shorn of all special distinctions, by the side of those of my countrymen who, for their so-called insignificance, are liable to suffer a degradation not fit for human beings".

TAGORE'S PUBLICATIONS

1. *Shiksar Herpher* (Our Education and Its Incongruities)

2. *Shiksha Samasya* (The Problem of Education)
3. *Abaran* (Culture or Covering)
4. *Tapovan* (Forest Colony)
5. *Dharmashiksha* (Religious Education)
6. *Hindu Visvavidyalaya* (Hindu University)
7. *Strishiksha* (Women Education)
8. *Shiksar Bahan* (The Vehicle of Education)
9. *My School*
10. *Shiksar Milan* (The Meeting of Cultures)
11. *A Poet's School*
12. *Shiksar Vikiran* (Diffusion of Education)
13. *Ashramer Shiksha* (Education in Ashram)
14. *Bodher Sadhana* (Education of the Feeling)
15. *Several Convocation Addresses*

FACTORS INFLUENCING TAGORE'S PHILOSOPHY OF EDUCATION

Tagore combined the elements of idealism, naturalism and pragmatism.

His philosophy of education was influenced by the following factors:

1. Influence of the Home Environment.
2. Influence of the School Environment.
3. Love for Nature.
4. His Extensive Visits.

Influence of the Home Environment: Tagore was born in a family in which the time-honoured ways of Indian life and tradition of the land were strictly adhered to. His father taught him ancient Indian literature. He set before the family the Indian ideals by the example of his own life, by his talks and writings. After leaving the school, Rabindranath Tagore spent a good deal of his time in the company of his father. This constant companionship of his father exerted a great influence on his life.

His Extensive Travels: His wide travels and visits to different countries of the world and his contacts with people of different nations, developed in him a faith in the brotherhood of man and spiritual unity of humanity.

Impact of School Environment: By nature, Tagore had a love for nature. His love for naturalism was strengthened on account of the artificial and unnatural environment of the schools he attended.

Tagore's life in the school was not happy. He felt himself like 'a parrot in the cage'. Tagore was unable to adjust himself to the 'dead routine and the teaching' of the educational institutions. His teachers pronounced that he was 'unfit' for studies. Tagore considered himself 'fortunate to escape' from these 'book learning factories'. He observed later on "The Masters and Pandits who were charged with my education soon abandoned the thankless task… and realised that this boy could never be driven along the beaten track of learning".

Tagore considered school a place of great discomfort, "There was no particular trouble in the school. Yet after all, it was a school. The rooms were pitiless, its walls stood like sentries. There was nothing like a home in it, it was like a big box with many compartments".

Traditional school to him was like a 'prison house'. He observed, "It was more like a pigeon-holed box. The time spent had been thoroughly wasted". About his teachers he wrote, "Of the teachers, I remember only one, whose language was so foul that, out of sheer contempt for him, I steadily refused to answer any one of his questions". Further he said, "I learnt about all the injustice, impatience, anger and partiality underlying the process of instruction, more easily than my lessons". The school according to him was "completely isolated from the surrounding life and beauty". It was a "restless nightmare like a jail… the whole thing was depressed".

All this made him a naturalist.

Impact of Tagore's Extensive Travel: Tagore spent considerable part of his life in travelling several parts of the world. This developed a pragmatic and rational outlook in him.

TAGORE'S VIEWS ON VARIOUS ASPECTS OF EDUCATION IN HIS OWN WORDS

Meaning of Education: Education is nothing short of the highest purpose of man—the fullest growth and freedom of soul.

Tagore's Thought of Education,
'Visvabharati Quarterly', Vol. XII, Part I—1946.

Object of Education: The object of education is to give man the unity of truth. We devote our sole attention to giving children information, not knowing that by this emphasis we are accentuating a break between the intellectual, physical and the spiritual life.

'Personality', p. 126.

Education for Knowing Oneself: The great use of education is not merely to collect facts but to know man and make oneself known to man.

'Rabindra Rachnavali', Vol. XII

Freedom of Mind as the Object of Education: I believe that the object of education is the freedom of mind which can be achieved through the path of freedom.

'Personality', p. 147.

Moral Education: I believe in the hour of meditation, and I must set aside fifteen minutes in the morning and fifteen minutes in the evening for that purpose. I insist on this period of meditation, not however, expecting the boy to be hypocrites and to make believe they are meditating. But I do insist that they remain quiet, that they exert the power of self-control.

'Personality' p. 145.

Vision and Reality: Education in all its different forms and channels has its ultimate purpose in the evolving of a luminous sphere of human mind from the nebula that has been rushing round ages to find itself an eternal centre of unity.

'Personality' p. 80.

Living Contact between the Teacher and the Taught

Communication of life can only be through a living agency. And culture, which is the life of mind, can only be imparted through man to man. Book-learning or scriptural texts may merely make us pedants. They are static and quantitative; they accumulate and are hoarded up under strict guards. Culture grows and moves and multiplies itself in life.

Discipline: For Tagore, an educational institution is "an open house in which students and teachers are one. They must live their compact life together." He observes that an educational institution "must not be a dead cage in which living minds are fed with food artificially prepared." He further remarks that "students are not dancing monkeys or bears." About the discipline of the educational institution he founded, he states, "I never said to them: Don't do this, or don't do that. The boys were encouraged to manage their own affairs."

Curriculum: Tagore was for a curriculum which should satisfy child's aesthetic, creative, spiritual and vocational needs. In his experimental school at Shantiniketan, Science (especially the experimental science) was taught to children in various classes. Shantiniketan school had a very well-equipped laboratory for performing experiments whereas in other schools, people had not even thought of this subject. Nature-study was also taught here, right in the midst of nature.

Methods of Teaching: Tagore strongly criticised the bookish and examination-oriented teaching. He stressed movement of the whole body in various learning activities. He followed the activity principle, and advocated constructive and creative activities. He believed that there should be daily practice by the pupils in expressing immediately what they are learning. The central point in educational activity according to Tagore, is joy which should pervade all types of activities. "Work should be wedded to joy". Tagore also emphasised the principle of curiosity and interest, and the spirit of play. He advocated fullness of experience-physical, mental, aesthetic and emotional. All this truly accords with the modern pedagogy.

Role of the Teacher: Tagore laid great emphasis on the attitude of the teacher. He wrote, "I have found that little children learn more quickly the attitude of the teacher than the knowledge imparted by him."

Tagore felt, "Most teachers do not know that in order to teach boys they have to be boys. Unfortunately, schoolmasters are obsessed with the consciousness of their dignity as grown up persons and as learned men, and therefore they always try to burden the children with their grown up manners and their learned manners, and that hurts the mind of the students unnecessarily." His concept of a good teacher is stated in these words, "A teacher can never truly teach unless he is still learning himself. A lamp can never light another lamp unless it continues to burn its own flame. The teacher who has come to the end of his subject, who has no living traffic with his knowledge, but merely repeats his lesson to his students, can only load their minds; he cannot quicken them. Truth not only must inform but also inspire."

In the final analysis, we must inevitably conclude that education can be imparted only by a teacher and never by a method.

Man can learn only from a man. Just as a water tank can be filled only with water and fire can be kindled only with fire, life can be inspired only with life.... In our social organisation we are searching for a guru who will add meaning and give pace to our life; in our educational system we are searching for a guru who will seek deliverance of our mind from its imprisonment. However, it may be, we want a human being in every sphere of our life. Mere a method shall bring us no salvation.

(*Siksa*, 1342, B.S.Ed., p. 286).

CONCEPT OF AN IDEAL SCHOOL

A Poet's School is an important writing showing the place of Nature in life and education. Children have the gift of freshness of senses. They can become natural with Nature and human with the human society. 'For our perfection we have to be vitally savage and mentally civilised.' But the misery is that a child is offered crowded solitude in a city where man is everywhere, with never a gap for the immense non-human, the Nature. The inexpensive power to be happy that the children bring to this world is 'Constantly worn away by friction with the brick-and-mortar arrangement of life.' The city-built education does not take heed of the non-civilised in us, which thirst for colour, for music, for the movement of life. This is why Tagore tried his best to develop in the children of his school 'the freshness of their feeling for nature, a sensitiveness of soul in their relationship with their human surrounding'.

He pointed out the great significance of the school atmosphere in the life of children whose mind, like the tree, has the power to gather food and nourishment from its surroundings. The cultural atmosphere keeps the mind sensitive to rich racial inheritance, glorious traditions and concentrated wisdom of ages. The school atmosphere must also develop sensitiveness of soul and allow freedom to the mind from bondage of ignorance and apathy.

An ideal school, according to Tagore, should have the following characteristics, and he attempted to introduce these elements in his school at Bolpur, located at a distance of about one hundred miles from Calcutta. Later on this school became Shantiniketan and grew into 'Visvabharati'.

1. The school should be situated in natural surroundings. There should prevail the atmosphere of nature's own beauty with her varied gifts of colours and dance, flowers and fruits, with the joy of her mornings and the peace of her starry nights.
2. It should provide an environment after the fashion of ancient '*Tapovans*' – forest schools about which he had read so much in the Upanishads.
3. It should give spiritual training to the students.
4. It should help the children in the cultivation of love of nature and sympathy with all living creatures.
5. It should educate children by providing an atmosphere of freedom.

6. It should educate children by making them alive to their natural surroundings.
7. It should educate children by providing an environment of living aspiration, based upon living contact between the teacher and the taught.
8. It should impart knowledge to children through mother tongue.
9. The school should provide for manual labour.
10. It should provide for close personal contact with the teacher. The number of students in classes should be very small.
11. There should be a well-equipped library.
12. It should be a community school where there is no distinction of caste and creed.
13. It should teach crafts like sewing, book-binding, weaving, carpentry etc.
14. It should include drawing, art and music as an integral part of the curriculum.
15. It should provide students adequate opportunities for choosing their hobbies and occupations.
16. It should be a self-governing institution—has a dairy farm, post office, hospital and workshop. Students hold their own courts.

VISVABHARATI AT SHANTINIKETAN IN NATURAL SURROUNDINGS

Rabindranath Tagore was not a dreamer. He was a great educational practitioner who himself was closely associated with the entire educational practices at Visvabharati.

The word Visvabharati is composed of two words. In Sanskrit, the word *Visva* means 'world' and *bharti* means 'culture'. Thus 'Visvabharati' would mean 'world culture'. The motto of this University is '*Yatra Visvam Bhavati Ekamidam*', i.e., where the world meets in one place. Through the Visvabharati as a whole, the poet and the seer sought "to establish a relationship between East and West, to promote inter-cultural and inter-social amity and understanding and fulfill the highest mission of the present age—the unification of mankind".

The Visvabharati was formally founded on 22nd December 1921. But it was not a new institution. It had grown gradually out of the Shantiniketan Ashrama. Today this 'Visvabharati' is known not only all over the world, but also attracts scholars from different parts of the world.

Tagore has observed, "I have formed the nucleus of an International University, as one of the best means of promoting mutual understanding between the East and the West." It was intended to be, "Treasure of Light" not only for India but also for the world.

Tagore wanted to extend by degrees the scope of this university on simple lines, until it comprehended the whole range of eastern culture—the Aryans, Semitic, Mongolian etc. Its object was to reveal the eastern mind to the world.

Main Features of Visvabharati

Tagore describes these as:

1. The institution that bore the name of Visvabharati was founded with the call that man had to be set free not only in the field of Nature but also among mankind.
2. The greatest distinction of our school is the direct and immediate emotional contact of pupils with their teachers and with external nature.
3. A speciality of our institution is that it wants to bring up our pupils in inseparable association with Nature.
4. It wants to hold before the world the ideal of the universality of man.
5. It is intended not only to be the intellectual centre of the intellectual life of India but also the centre of her economic life.
6. It is envisaged to be the nucleus of an international university and as one of the means of promoting mutual understanding between the East and the West.

Natural Environment at Shantiniketan

Education is imparted in the lap of natural surroundings. The influence of green trees, open fields, seasonal skies, songs and chirpings of birds and other natural phenomena, fills the pupils' mind with spiritual elevation. Tagore himself says, "Having in my mind the ideal of a school, which should be a home and a temple in one, where teaching should be a part of worshipful life. I selected this spot far away from all distraction of the town, hallowed by the memory of a pious life, whose days were passed here in communion with God."

Institutions at Visvabharati

Following institutions were started to carry out his experiments in education:

1. Sisu Bhavan (Nursery School)
2. Path Bhavan (School Section—Matriculation Examination)
3. Siksha Bhavan (Higher Secondary)
4. Vidya Bhavan (College of Undergraduate and Post-Graduate Studies and Research)
5. Vinya Bhavan (College of Teaching)
6. Kala Bhavan (College of Fine Arts and Crafts)
7. Sangit Bhavan (College of Dance)
8. Sriniketan (Department of Rural Reconstruction)
9. Siksa Satra (Rural High School)
10. Silpa Sadana (College of Industrial Training)
11. Cheena Bhavan (School of Languages, e.g., Chinese, Tibetan, etc.)

By and large, all formed part of Visvabharati University

TAGORE'S CONTRIBUTION TO EDUCATION

Tagore's concept of education and its practices balance the claims of different schools of educational philosophy, i.e., humanism, idealism, naturalism, pragmatism, realism and supernaturalism. His philosophy is a true blend of the Eastern and Western philosophy.

The Visvabharati is the embodiment of his educational ideals.

Tagore is one of the very few educational philosophers whose philosophy is the outcome of his educational experiments. Simultaneously, he gave a practical shape to his ideology.

Rabindranath was a great educational practitioner. He was not a dreamer only to leave behind a legacy of the principles of life. He worked them out in a constructive way.

Setting up educational institutions in natural surroundings and the environment of freedom from fear – the two principal features of his theory and practice of education bear the mark of his naturalism.

11

Philosophical Thought of Gandhiji (1869-1948)

BRIEF LIFE SKETCH OF GANDHIJI

Mohandas Karam Chand Gandhi (Karam Chand was his father), popularly known as 'Bapu', out of affection and reverence by the people, 'Mahatma', on account of his saintly nature and 'Father of the Nation' for the regeneration of the Indian nation, free from the British rule was a great educator, a nation builder, a political leader, a social worker, a statesman and a writer. Gandhiji had a charismatic appeal and he attracted thousands of devoted workers hailing from all sections of the society. He took up cases which ultimately touched the life of the common man.

Early Life and Education: Gandhiji was born on October 2, 1869 at Porbandar in Gujarat. His father was a Dewan (Chief Administrator and Chief Revenue Officer) of a small state. At school, he was slow, hesitant and shy. He was married to Kasturba at the age of thirteen. His mother was very pious and he was greatly influenced by her.

Education in England: When 18 years old, he was sent to London to study law where he remained for three years. His mother made him promise that in England, he would not take meat and alcohol and indulge in sex. Gandhiji kept his promise.

Work in South Africa: After returning from England, he started his law practice at Bombay. However, he was not very successful.

In April, 1893, he went to South Africa in connection with a civil law case of a firm. In 1893 itself, he was thrown out of a first class compartment in Durban (South Africa) for he was a coloured man. He stayed there for about 20 years. This was a turning point in his life. Gandhiji found that the Indians in South Africa were treated very cruelly and in fact like animals. They had no political rights. Gandhiji took up cases which were not entirely political but touched intimately the life of the people. Gandhiji gave up his legal practice. He completely devoted himself to the service of the people. He put into practice '*Satyagraha*' and '*Ahimsa*'.

GANDHIJI'S PUBLICATIONS ON EDUCATION

Important publications on education and having bearing on education are:

1. *My Experiments with Truth.* (Autobiography)
2. *Basic Education*
3. *Towards New Education*
4. *True Education*
5. *To the Students*
6. *Task Before Indian Students*
7. *India of My Dreams*
8. *Medium of Instruction*
9. *Tasks fore India*

Gandhiji also wrote extensively on education in '*Harijan*' – a paper founded by him.

PRINCIPAL FEATURES OF GANDHIJI'S PHILOSOPHY OF LIFE

1. *Supreme God*: He said, "God pervades everything. God is life, Truth and Light".
2. *Truth and Ahimsa* (*Non-violence*): According to Gandhiji, "Truth and *Ahimsa* are the two sides of a coin. They

are intertwined and it is practically impossible to separate them". '*Satyagraha*' implies holding of truth, through love and purity.

3. *Service of Humanity*: Gandhiji observed, "The immediate service of all human beings becomes a necessary part because it is the only way to see Him in His creation".
4. *Self-discipline and Self-purification*: Gandhiji always held the high ideals of purity, sacrifice and service.
5. *Righteousness and Truth as the Highest Religion*: Gandhiji was of the firm view that 'true religion and true morality are inseparably bound up with each other'.
6. *Ram Rajya as the Concept of a Society*: He wanted to establish *Ram Rajya* which he identified with justice, peace, happiness and welfare of all.

According to Gandhiji, man's ultimate aim is the realisation of God and all his endeavour—political, religious and social—must be guided to this end, "The immediate service of all human beings becomes a necessary part of the endeavour, simply because the only way to find God is to see *Him* in *His* creation and be one with it—I am a part and parcel of the whole and I cannot find *Him* apart from the rest of humanity." For Gandhiji, God lives in the temple of humanity and man becomes great exactly in the degree in which he works for the welfare of his fellow men.

FACTORS THAT INFLUENCED GANDHIJI'S PHILOSOPHY OF LIFE AND PHILOSOPHY OF EDUCATION

Following were the chief influences which had a great effect on Gandhiji's philosophy of life and philosophy of education:

1. *Mother's Influence*: Gandhiji's mother taught him the lessons of simplicity and piety.

2. *Three Great Thinkers*.

(i) Rayachand Bhai Patel who taught Gandhiji the first lesson in non-violence.

(ii) Ruskin, through his book *Unto the Last* drew his attention to the principle of dignity of labour.

(iii) Leo Tolstoy's *The Kingdom of the God is within You,* greatly influenced his spiritual outlook.

3. *The Phoenix Settlement* (South Africa) where Gandhiji conducted early experiments

4. *The Tolstoy Farm*: In 1911, Gandhiji started an Ashram in Transwal. It was here that Gandhiji helped children in their all-round development. He taught vocations such as cooking, digging and massage work. The medium of instruction was mother-tongue. English was also taught. Children learnt by doing. Textbooks were not used. No punishment was administered. Creed of non-violence was put into practice in letter and spirit.

5. *The Sabarmati Ashram*: After returning to India in 1914, Gandhiji started the Sabarmati Ashram. A school was attached with the Ashram which Gandhiji wanted to make a model school.

THOUGHTS OF GANDHIJI ON VARIOUS DIMENSIONS OF EDUCATION IN HIS OWN WORDS

Meaning of Education

Real Education has to draw out the best from the boys and girls to be educated. This can never be done by packing ill-assorted and unwanted information into the heads of the students. It becomes a dead weight crushing all originality in them and turning them into mere automata.

('*Harijan*', December 1, 1933)

By education I mean an all-round drawing out of the best in child and man—body, mind and spirit.

('*Harijan*', July 31, 1937)

Literacy is not the end of education not even the beginning. It is only one of the means whereby man and women can be educated. Literacy in itself is no education.

('*Harijan*', July 31, 1937)

I would develop in the child his hands, his brain and his soul. ('*Basic Education*', p. 23)

Purity of personal life is the one indispensable condition for building a sound education.

('*Towards New Education*', p. 31)

I hold that true education of the intellect can only come through a proper exercise and training of the bodily organs, e.g., hands, feet, eyes, ears, nose, etc.

('*Basic Education*', p. 123)

True education is that which draws out and stimulates the spiritual, the intellectual and physical faculties of the children.

(Tendulkar, '*Mahatma*', Vol. IV, p. 187)

Education and Character

The end of all knowledge must be building up character. What is education without character and what is character without elementary purity? ('*Towards New Education*', p. 301)

All our learning of recitation of the Vedas, correct knowledge of Sanskrit, Latin and Greek and what not, will avail as nothing if they do not enable us to cultivate purity of heart. The end of all knowledge may be the building of character. ('*True Education*', p. 229)

The Teacher

Woe to the teacher who teaches one thing with the lips and carries another in the heart. ('*To the Students*', p. 16)

The politician may succeed in his purpose even though he lacks character, but a pupils' teacher cannot do without character. If he lacks, he will be like salt without its savour.

('*True Education*', p. 161)

I always felt that the true textbook for the pupils is his teacher. ('*Autobiography*', p. 41)

It is possible for a teacher living miles away to affect the spirit of the pupils by his way of living.

('*Towards New Education*', p. 44)

Education Through Craft

I want the whole process of education to be imparted through some handicraft or industry.(*'Basic Education'*, p. 191)

My idea is not to teach a particular profession or occupation to the children, but to develop the full man through teaching that occupation. (Tendulkar, *'Mahatma'*, Vol. IV, p. 200)

The brain must be educated through hand.

(*'Basic Education'*, p. 190)

The old idea was to add a craft to the ordinary curriculum of education followed in the schools. That is to say, the craft was to be taken in hand wholly separate from education. To me that seems a fatal mistake. The teacher must learn the craft and correlate his knowledge to the craft, so that he will impart all that knowledge to his pupils through the medium of the particular craft that he chooses.

Take the instance of spinning. Unless I know arithmetic I cannot report how many yards of yarn I have produced on the 'takli'. I must learn addition and subtraction and multiplication and division. In dealing with complicated sums, I shall have to use symbols and so I get my algebra. Even here, I would insist on the use of Hindustani letters instead of Roman.

Takli-spinning leads me into the History of East India Company.

There is no limit to the possibilities of knowledge that can be imparted through this medium.

(*'Harijan'*, February 18, 1939)

Methods of Teaching

It is not by making our brains a store-house for cramming facts that our understanding is opened. An intelligent approach to an industrial training is often a more valuable aid to the intellect than an indifferent reading of literature.

Pupils should know to discriminate between what should be received and what rejected. It is the duty of the teacher to teach his pupils discrimination.

(*'Towards New Education'*, p. 34)

The utterly false idea that intelligence can be developed only through book-reading should give place to the truth that the quickest development of the mind can be achieved by artisan's work being learnt in a scientific way.

(Bose, Nirmal Kumar, *'Selections from Gandhiji'*, p. 288)

The brain must be educated through the hand.

(*'Harijan'*, Feb. 29, 1939)

The core of my suggestion is that handicrafts are to be taught not merely for production work but for developing the intellect. (*'Basic Education'*, p. 44)

I want to teach through hand-work all the subjects like History, Geography, Arithmetic, Science, Language, Painting etc. (Tendulkar, *'Mahatma'*, Vol. IV, p. 196)

Freedom and Discipline

The students mind must not be caged. This does not mean that they are not subject to discipline. No school can be run without it. But discipline has nothing to do with artificial restraint upon students' all-round growth.

(*'True Education'*, p. 57)

I have always been opposed to corporal punishment.

(*'Towards New Education'*, p. 19)

GANDHIJI'S DISSATISFACTION WITH THE EXISTING SYSTEM OF EDUCATION AND FORMULATION OF BASIC SYSTEMS OF EDUCATION

Gandhiji realised that the prevailing system of education was unreal and outdated. He observed, "I am convinced that the present system of education is not only wasteful but positively harmful. Most of the boys are lost to the parents and to the occupations to which they were born. They pick up evil habits, effect urban ways and get a smattering of something which may be anything but education".

Gandhiji further observed, "The present system of education does not meet the requirements of the country in any shape or form. English has been made medium of education in all the highest branches of learning, and it has created a permanent bar between the highly educated few and the uneducated many".

Gandhiji went on to criticise the system. "We have up to now concentrated on stuffing children's minds with all kinds of information without even thinking or stimulating or developing them".

Gandhiji accordingly stressed, "Let us now cry a halt and concentrate on educating the child properly through manual work not as a side activity but as a prime means of intellectual activity".

Main Features of the Systems of Education based on Gandhiji's Philosophy

1. Education for a just social order.
2. Education through craft and manual work.
3. Education through mother tongue.
4. Self-sufficient education.
5. Education related to life activities and experiences.
6. Dignity of labour.
7. Correlation.
8. Religious education.
9. Spiritual training.
10. Freedom to children but under discipline.
11. Character development.
12. Mass education.
13. Women education.

ORIGIN OF BASIC EDUCATION/ *NAI TALEM* / WARDHA SCHEME OR SYSTEM OF EDUCATION

The origin of Basic System of Education may be traced back to July 1937 when Gandhiji wrote in '*Harijan*' (a journal started by him), "By education, I mean an all-round development drawing out of the best in child and man—body, mind and spirit.

Literacy itself is no education. I would, therefore, begin the child's education by teaching it a useful handicraft and enabling it to produce from the moment it begins its training. Thus every school can be made self-supporting, the condition being that the state takes over the manufacture of these schools".

In October, 1937 a Conference of National Workers was held at Wardha under the chairmanship of Mahatma Gandhi. His ideas were considered and the following resolutions passed:

1. That in the opinion of this Conference free and compulsory education be provided for seven years on a nation-wide scale.
2. That the medium of instruction be the mother-tongue.
3. That the Conference endorses the proposal made by Mahatma Gandhi, that the process of education throughout this period should centre round some productive form of manual labour, and that all other abilities to be developed, or training to be given should, as far as possible, be integrally related to the environment of the child.
4. That the Conference expects that the system of education will gradually be able to cover the remuneration of teachers.

Zakir Hussain Committee on Basic Education: Formulation of the Scheme

The Conference appointed a Committee under the chairmanship of Dr. Zakir Hussain, a renowned educationist. The report of this Committee was published in 1938. The report is known as Wardha Scheme of Education. The scheme was approved by Mahatma Gandhi and accepted by the Indian National Congress.

CURRICULUM OF BASIC EDUCATION AS IT EMERGED IN DUE COURSE

The fundamental features of the scheme that emerged after changes are as follows:

1. A school of say 5½ hours could roughly be divided on the following basis:

Physical activities	20 minutes
Mother Tongue	20 minutes
Social Studies & General Science	60 minutes
Art	40 minutes
Arithmetic	20 minutes
Craft work including study of correlated subjects	2½ hours

2. Free and compulsory education to be given for 8 years (from 6 to 14 years) in two stages. The junior stage to cover five years and the senior 3 years.
3. The medium of instruction is to be the mother tongue.
4. Education is to centre round some form of productive work. The social and physical environment to be used for correlation in addition to craft.
5. The self-supporting aspect not to be over-emphasised. The sale-proceeds of the finished goods to be able to help the school to cover some part of its expenditure.
6. External examinations to be abolished. The day-to-day work of the students to be the determining factor.
7. Text-books to be avoided as far as possible.
8. Cleanliness and health, citizenship, play and recreation to be given sufficient importance.

TENETS/MERITS OF BASIC EDUCATION/CHIEF FEATURES

Following are the tenets of Basic Education:

1. *Craft as the Core of the Basic Plan*: Craft is the medium of education in the basic system. Gandhiji writes, "The core of my suggestion is that handicrafts are not to be taught merely for productive work but for developing the intellect of the pupils". According to his view "stress should be laid on the principles of cooperative activity, planning, accuracy, initiative and individual responsibility in learning". According to him, "the process of education should be imparted through some handicraft or industry".

2. *Self-supporting Aspect*: "Earn while you learn" is another feature of the plan. The idea of a self-sufficient basic school has a special significance in a poor country like India. Without self-sufficient schools it is very doubtful if we could fulfil the obligation to our Constitution of providing free and compulsory education to all the boys and girls of school-going age. In the absence of such schools, we may have to wait for many decades to provide education to such a group.

3. *Integrated Knowledge*: Basic education treats knowledge as an integrated whole. Curriculum is built round three integrally related centres: (i) Physical environment, (ii) Social environment, and (iii) Craft work.

4. *Relationship with Life*: A basic school must become an active environment where teaching is not cut off from the life of the miniature community of the school and the community itself. Education is to be directed to the needs of life. It is not to pursue an idea which has no relation with or is totally isolated from the real situations of life.

5. *Learning by Doing*: Learning by doing sums up the educational methods of basic education. It is absolutely wrong to think that true education is acquired from books alone. There are other methods and sources which are more helpful in acquiring true knowledge. 'Chalk' and 'Talk' lessons are also not very useful. All educationists have condemned bookish knowledge. Gandhiji believed that school must be a 'doing thing'. In basic system of education children acquire the knowledge of the formal school subjects as a by-product of purposeful activities.

6. *Training in Citizenship*: Basic education aims at developing ideas of mutual understanding and habits of cooperative and mutually helpful living among the students through its various practical and constructive programmes. The new education aims at giving the citizens of the future a keen sense of personal warmth, dignity and efficiency. It is likely to strengthen in them the desire for self-improvement and social service in a cooperative community.

7. *Free and Compulsory Education for Eight Years*: By free and compulsory education, we mean an education for which parents

will not have to pay any fee and for which they must send their children to school. Gandhiji writes, "Primary education extending over a period of 7 years or longer, and covering all the subjects up to the matriculation standard except English, plus a vocation used as a vehicle for drawing out the minds of boys and girls in all departments of knowledge should take the place of what passes today under the name of primary, middle and high school education". In due course it was accepted that the duration of free and compulsory education should be for a period of 8 years.

8. *Emphasis on Mother-tongue*: Gandhiji stressed that proper education can only be imparted through the mother-tongue. Foreign language as the medium of instruction makes us unfit for original work. It makes us crammers and imitators. Dr. Zakir Hussain Committee observes, "The proper teaching of mother-tongue is the foundation of all education. Without the capacity to speak effectively and to read and write correctly and lucidly, no one can develop precision of thought or clarity of ideas. Moreover, it is a means of introducing the child to the rich heritage of his people's ideas, emotions and aspirations and can, therefore, be made a valuable means of social education, whilst also instilling right ethical and moral values. Also, it is a natural outlet for the expression of the child's aesthetic sense and application and if the proper approach is adopted the study of literature becomes a source of joy and creative appreciation."

9. *Greater Freedom for the Teacher and the Taught*: In basic education discipline does not mean order and external restraint but an intelligent use of freedom. The teacher gets many opportunities to make experiments, think for himself and put his ideas and plans into practice.

10. *Basic Education as a Means of Social Equality*: The ultimate objective of basic education is to create a social order in which there is no unnatural division between 'haves' and have-nots' and every one is assured of a living wage and the right to freedom.

11. *Basic Education in the Rural as Well as in Urban Area*: It is wrong to assume that basic education is intended to be imparted in the rural area only. "In fact, in one sense there is a

greater need for basic education in urban areas than in rural areas. In rural areas the children who participate in the life of the farm or allied occupation of their families have certain types of further education. In performing their jobs the children come into direct contact with actual life, and the experience they get forms the basis of further education. On the other hand, in large towns and big industrial cities the children miss the opportunities for rich experiences and direct contact with life", observed Dr. K.L. Shrimali. Basic education is a plan of national education for the whole country including both rural as well as urban areas. Keeping in view the educative possibilities of a craft in relation to local needs, curriculum may differ from region to region. There is no rigidity in the curriculum of basic education. It would be wrong to think that rural children should have altogether a different type of education from urban children. Difference will be of a degree and not of kind. Basic principles of life are the same everywhere.

Significance of the Word 'Basic'

The word 'Basic' is derived from the word 'Base' which means the bottom or the foundation of a thing upon which the whole thing rests or is made.

It is basic because it is based on ancient Indian culture.

It is basic because it lays down the minimum educational standards which every Indian child is entitled to receive without any distinction of caste or creed.

It is basic because it is closely related to the basic needs and interests of the child.

It is basic because it makes use of the native potentialities of the child.

It is basic because it is intimately related to the basic occupations of the community.

It is basic because it is for the common man of the country, who is the foundation and the backbone of our national life.

It is basic because it comes first in time, i.e. it is the primary period of one's education.

CRITICISM OF BASIC EDUCATION

1. *Based on Unsound Psychological Foundations*: P.S. Naidu has observed, "The delicate but inexorable laws governing the development of the tender mind of the child have been completely ignored. The child is treated just as a policeman or a soldier, merely as a unit in a homogeneous mass. His individuality is ignored. He is viewed merely as a means to an end – the end being earning capacity and citizenship of sorts". He has further stated, "Play is the only means by which creative energy can be released. Enlightened and informed educational opinion all over the civilised world is decidedly against forcing the child to learn a craft before he is twelve plus. It is nothing short of cruelty to make the child earn an anna or half per hour during the stage when he ought to be playing and enjoying himself."

2. *Deficiency of Craft as the Primary Basis of Correlation*: The critics point out that it is impossible to establish any natural and real correlation between craft and all the subjects. "It is absurd to hang all knowledge from the peg of a single craft."

3. *Basic Education not Suited in an Age of Industrialisation*: As ours is a system of education which claims to produce an integrated individual, the emphasis on craft is out of place in a community which has its face turned towards developing its economy to the full. Basic education failed to relate to the economic policy of the State. But if this point is ignored, we shall find ourselves burdened with an educational system which turns out misfits even more rapidly than the one with which we are so dissatisfied. It is stated that with rapid industrialisation of India, knowledge of science and mathematics may become more desirable than skill in handicrafts.

4. *Ruinous Competition*: This scheme hits the professional artisans hard by creating ruinous competitions.

5. *Deficient Working of Basic Schools*: In the words of J. Lahri, "There is some loss in mechanical arithmetic and spelling lack of sufficient intensive and repetitive drill".

6. *Neglect of the Child*: "In a hurry to pay more attention to craft, it has neglected the child".

"Basic education is looked upon more as a social and economic duty than as a joyful adventure".

7. *Faulty Teaching of Craft*: "Craft is only a slogan, a fiction, which is practised on ceremonial occasions for the benefit of visitors".

8. *Faulty Time-table*: In a basic school nearly half the normal time is given to academic education, the rest being taken up by crafts. And further, since on the time-table academic subjects generally come after the craft work, mostly agriculture, students are sometimes too tired to take to academic work seriously.

9. *No Dexterity in Any Craft*: R.K. Singh has observed, "Students spend one-third or half the time for craft work without acquiring any dexterity worth speaking of in any craft."

10. *Neglect of Religion Education*: There is no place for religious instruction in the curriculum of basic education.

Some Epithets Attached with Basic System of Education

1. *Basic Education is a Fad*: It has no sound psychological and pedagogical basis.
2. *Basic Education is a Fallacy*: The very fundamentals are wrong and not properly conceived.
3. *Basic Education is a Farce*: The scheme is impracticable. Traditional methods are still followed. The craft materials are just stored and a show is put up, whenever there are visitors.
4. *Basic Education is a Fraud*: It is a sort of political stunt to play with the sentiments of the people.

FUTURE OF BASIC EDUCATION AND THE EDUCATION COMMISSION (1964-66)

The Commission believed that the essential elements of basic education were fundamentally sound, but some modifications were needed: The movement of basic education launched by Mahatma Gandhi before independence, proposing a new type of elementary education for the nation which would centre round some form of manual and productive work and have intimate links with the life of the community, was a landmark in the history of education in India. It was a revolt against the sterile, book-centred examination-oriented system of education that had developed along traditional lines during several decades of British rule. It created a national ferment, which may not have transformed the quality of education at the primary stage, but which has certainly left its impact on educational thought and practice on a much wider sphere. "We believe that the essential elements of the system are fundamentally sound, and that with necessary modification these can form part of education, not only at the primary stage but at all stages in our national system. These elements are: (1) productive activity in education; (2) correlation of the curriculum with the productive activity and the physical and social environment; and (3) intimate contact between the school and the local community."

The Commission popularised the concept of "work experience" and saw that two ideas—"work experience" and "basic education"—were essentially similar.

"In the curricula of most contemporary school system, particularly in the socialist countries of Europe, a place is found for what is variously called 'manual work' or 'work experience'. In our country, a revolutionary experiment was launched by Mahatma Gandhi in the form of basic education. The concept of work experience was essentially similar. It may be described as a redefinition of his educational thinking in terms of a society launched on the road to industrialisation".

The Commission gave a call for the reorientation of the basic education programme in view of the changed character and need of the new society. It is not difficult to miss the clear shift of emphasis in terms of a new science-oriented social order in the following words:

"The programme of basic education did involve work-experience for all children in the primary schools, though the activities proposed were concerned with the indigenous crafts and the village employment patterns. If in practice basic education has become largely frozen around certain crafts, there is no denying the fact that it always stressed the vital principle of relating education to productivity. What is now needed is a reorientation of the basic education programme to the needs of a society that has to be transformed with the help of science and technology. In other words, work experience must be forward-looking in keeping with the character of the new social order".

SUMMING UP: THE PHILOSOPHY OF GANDHIJI AND ITS IMPACT ON EDUCATION

It is not quite fair to limit Gandhiji's philosophy and principles of education to basic system of education. His contribution goes far beyond. Basic system of education is just one of his contributions to education. There is no dimension of life and education on which Gandhiji has not expressed his views. His views on the importance of mother tongue as medium of instruction, his emphasis on manual labour, his stress on 'Learning by Earning', his views on the significance of women education and the role of the teacher etc. are quite relevant today.

To Gandhiji, education was an integral part of a comprehensive programme of socio-economic reconstruction of Indian society.

As a political and spiritual leader and an economic and social reformer, Gandhiji was naturally concerned with education. All his constructive programmes, economic, educational, ethical, political, social and spiritual were organically interconnected. Gandhiji wrote, "My life is indivisible whole and all my activities run into one another, and they all have their rise in my insatiable love for mankind."

12

Sri Aurobindo (1872-1950): Integral Education

BRIEF LIFE SKETCH

Revolutionary and freedom fighter turned '*rishi*' (seer), Sri Aurobindo was born in an educated middle class family of Calcutta (Kolkata), West Bengal. Sri Aurobindo was a very brilliant student. At the age of 7, he went to England and spent there about 14 years. He received his education at Cambridge. Besides English, he mastered Latin and Greek, and learnt French, German, Italian and Spanish. At the age of 18, he passed the entrance examination of the coveted ICS [Indian Civil Service (ICS)] - the most coveted service. He, however, did not appear in the riding test, which was also compulsory. This was perhaps on account of his hatred for the foreign rule.

On return to India, he served as a professor of English at Baroda College. He learnt Bengali, Gujarati, Marathi and Sanskrit. He drank deep in the culture and philosophy of India.

Sri Aurobindo took an active part in the freedom struggle and courted arrest. He was a great pioneer in the National Education Movement, launched in the wake of agitation against the 'Partition of Bengal'. He joined as principal of Bengal National College of Calcutta (now Jadavpur University).

In 1910 he left political activities and went to Pondicherry (a French settlement in India at that time). He turned to the study of religious, philosophical and spiritual literature. He propounded the concept of the national system of education.

He set up an international Ashram and International Centre

of Education at Pondicherry and started several educational and social activities. He also started a new experiment known as Aurovill as a city of human unity.

Aurobindo's Important Publications on Education and Allied Subjects

1. *A System of National Education.*
2. *Sri Aurobindo and the Mother on Education.*
3. *The Human Cycle.*
4. *Ideal of Human Unity.*
5. *The Life Divine.*
6. *Riddle of the World.*
7. *The Savitri.*
8. *Essays on Geeta.*
9. *On the Vedas.*
10. *Eight Upanishads*

SELECT QUOTES OF SRI AUROBINDO ON EDUCATION

1. "To bring out the real man is the first business of education".
2. "The chief aim of education should be to help the growing soul to draw out which is best and make it perfect for a noble cause".
3. "The best method of moral education is by personal example, daily converse the books read from day-to-day".
4. "Perfect liberty would be desirable for the child".
5. "The teacher is not an instructor or task master, he is a helper and guide".
6. "Indeed if the education is to have its maximum result, it must begin even before birth".
7. "The true basis of education is the study of the human mind".
8. "The idea of hammering the child into the shape desired by the parent or teacher is a barbarous and ignorant superstition".

9. "The education of the intellect divorced from the perfection of the moral and emotional nature is injurious to human nature".

PROMINENT FEATURES OF AUROBINDO'S PHILOSOPHY

1. Everyone has in him something Divine.
2. The task is to find it, develop it and use it.
3. This Divine can be obtained by a spiritual discipline, called yoga.
4. Aurobindo's concept of yoga is not that of a *sanyasi* who turns away from life in order to turn towards God.
5. Yoga is for the ordinary man, while he carries on his worldly pursuits.
6. If a merchant wishes to follow yoga, he regards his work as Divine he does not use unfair practices to earn money.
7. If a student, looks for higher values, he must observe *Brahmacharya* (self-control).

SRI AUROBINDO'S MAIN IDEAS ON EDUCATION

1. Aims of Education

1. According to Sri Aurobindo, "The chief aim of education should be to help the growing soul to draw out which is best and make it perfect for a noble cause".
2. The education should enable an individual to realise his inner self which is a part of the universal consciousness. The individual has to enter into right relationships not only within himself but also with the people of his country and with the universal society to which he belongs.

The human race is composed of people or nations and a nation is composed of individuals. The nations make the universal humanity.

2. Functions of Education

Following are the chief functions of education:

(i) To bring out the real man.

(ii) To build the powers of the human mind and spirit, i.e., the evoking of knowledge, character and culture.

(iii) To enable the individual to establish a clear continuity between the past, present and the future.

(iv) To enable the individual to establish right relations with life.

3. Nature of the Child and Principles of Teaching

Sri Aurobindo attaches great importance to the divine gift inherent in the children. Accordingly he has stated the following three principles of teaching:

The first principle of true teaching is that nothing can be taught. The teacher is not an instructor or task master, he is a helper and guide.

The teacher's work is to suggest and not to impose on the mind of the students. He does not actually train the mind of his student but helps him to perfect his mind and encourages him in every way in this process. Thus he does not impart knowledge, but shows the way how knowledge can be acquired. Knowledge is within the pupil and the pupil has to help himself to bring it out, but he needs help. Somebody must tell him where it is and how it can be 'habituated to rise to the surface'. Teacher alone can do this work.

The second principle is that the mind has to be consulted in its growth. The idea of hammering the child into the shape desired by the parent or teacher is a barbarous and ignorant superstition. Sri Aurobindo wrote, "It is wrong and rather immoral to force adult will on the child. The divine in the child should not be ignored and mutilated. To force the nature of the child to abandon its own '*Dharma*' is to do permanent harm".

The third principle of teaching is to work from the near to the far, from the known to the unknown. Man's nature is moulded by his soul's past, his heredity and his environment. The past is the foundation, the present is the material and future is the aim and each must find its due and natural place in any national system of education.

4. Main Principles of Learning

(i) Concentration is the first principle of learning.
(ii) '*Abhyasa*' or steady natural practice is the second principle of learning.

5. Moral Education

This should be on the following methods:

(i) Personal examples of the teachers and elders.
(ii) Study of books having lofty examples.
(iii) '*Satsanga*' i.e., good company.
(iv) Suggesting and not commanding and imposing.

6. Discipline

'*Chitta Shuddhi*' i.e., purification of the mental and moral habits should be the basis of discipline. This means to discriminate between right and wrong impressions and to absorb right ones in the mind.

Sri Aurobindo advises teachers not to be arbitrary, despotic, impatient and ill tempered.

7. Physical Education

Perfection is the true aim of education and physical development is an integral part of perfection. Moreover without physical development, '*Dharma*' cannot be performed. Only a healthy body can contain a healthy mind. As the Sanskrit saying goes, '*Shariram khalu dharmasadhanam*' (the body is the means of fulfillment of *dharma*).

8. Curriculum

It should include the following:

(i) Physical development studies
(ii) Mental development studies
(iii) Cultural development studies
(iv) Vital sciences relating to preservation of body etc.

(v) Vocational development studies
(vi) International understanding programmes

9. Teacher—A Guide and Helper

Sri Aurobindo observes, "The teacher is not an instructor or task-master; he is a helper and guide. His business is to suggest and not to impose. He does not actually train the pupil's mind, he only shows him how to perfect his instruments of knowledge and helps and encourages him in the process. He does not impart knowledge to him; he shows him how to acquire knowledge for himself. He does not call forth the knowledge for himself. He does not call forth the knowledge that is within. He only shows him where it lies and how it can be habituated to rise to the surface".

NATIONAL SYSTEM OF EDUCATION

Prevailing Defects in Education: Shri Aurobindo found the following defects in the prevailing system of education:

1. It was denationalising.
2. It was degrading.
3. It was impoverishing the mind; soul and character.
4. It was bad in kind.

Main Characteristics of the National System of Education: Aurobindo pointed out the following elements:

(i) Human and spiritual values are complementary and supplementary.
(ii) Education does not become national by tagging the word 'national' to the system.
(iii) Education should pay due attention to modern knowledge and scientific progress.
(iv) Mere knowledge of science does not make us educated in the true sense. This must be related to powers of the human mind and spirit.

(v) There should be a balanced understanding of the national and international relationships of universal humanity.

INTEGRAL EDUCATION

Meaning of Integral Education

According to Sri Aurobindo, "Integral education is that which helps to bring out to full advantage, makes ready for the full purpose of life and scope of all that is in the individual man, which at the same time helps him to enter into his right relation with life, mind and soul of the people to which he belongs and with the great total life, mind and soul of humanity of which he himself is a unit and his people or nation, a separate and yet inseparable member".

The human body, mind and intellect combine together to form a magnificent machine; we call it a machine for want of a better world but it is superior to any other equipment built by man. Education must integrate these elements to serve its real purpose.

TWO-FOLD BASES OF INTEGRATED EDUCATION

1. Individuality is one whole.
2. Humanity is one. There are no inconsistencies in the East and the West.

1. Individuality is One Whole

(a) *Harmonious Development of Three Dimensions of Individuality*: Body, mind and soul have their significance when they are harmoniously developed as they constitute the whole individuality. Likewise individual's intellectual development must develop in relation to his moral, emotional and spiritual nature and vice versa. In other words integral education must develop all the dimensions of the individuality of the person. According to Sri Aurobindo, there should be a balanced and harmonious development of all the aspects of human personality-cognitive (knowledge), conative (skills) and affective (attitudes and values). An individual thus becomes an integrated individual.

(b) *Socio-economico-politico Integration*: Neither man has been regarded as a pre-eminently reasoning animal so that education should aim at developing only his mental capacities, nor has he been seen as an economic, political and social being only so that education should train him as a productive and disciplined member of the society. These, no doubt, are aspects and characteristics of human being but they do not define the whole of the real man. The real man is not only a bundle of selfish interests, nor alone an intellectual entity, nor merely a social being. He is something more. Beyond the physical and mental bounds there is spiritual existence. Sri Aurobindo said, "India has seen always in man the individual a soul, a portion of the divinity enwrapped in mind and body".

(c) *Different Aspects of the 'Self' but 'Self' is One*: Man is the conscious manifestation of the universal spirit. We may distinguish in man different aspects of his being, mental, intellectual, ethical, practical, aesthetic, physical and the like but all these have been as powers of a 'self' that manifests through them and yet they are not all the 'self'.

(d) *No Concentration on Academic Perfection Alone*: The study of mind is fundamental in education. Any system of education which concentrates on academic perfection of the child with disregard to his mind is destined to fail. It would rather hamper the intellectual growth than producing an integrated mind.

2. Oneness of Humanity

Sri Aurobindo immersed himself in Vedanta and Yoga. Instead of seeing conflict or finding inconsistencies between the East and the West, he evolved a synthesis of both. He also synthesised 'Spirit' and 'Matter', 'Science' and 'Vedanta'.

3. Multiple Cells

Sri Aurobindo considers all forms in the universe as multiple cells of one consciousness and the Yoga as the means through which one may come into contact with the true 'self' and unite the separate parts of oneself and also can see the divine in others.

4. Inner as Well as Outer Realisation

Aurobindo says that we must aim not only at an inner realisation but an outer realisation also—the establishment of the Kingdom of God not only within the heart but also in the world of human affairs.

TASK OF INTEGRAL EDUCATION

What really is the task of integral education? Sri Aurobindo said that there are three that education must take into account:

1. The man
2. The nation or people
3. Universal humanity

Education must enable us to understand the interrelationship among these three.

Stages or Phases of Integral Education

According to Aurobindo, education to be integral must have the following aspects relating to the five principal activities of the human being:

1. The physical
2. The vital
3. The mental
4. The psychic
5. The spiritual

Sri Aurobindo stated that usually these stages or phases of education succeed each other in a chronological order following the growth of the individual. This, however, does not mean that one stage should replace another until another is complete but that all must continue, complementing each other, till the end of life.

Five Stages or Phases of Integral Education

(1) Physical Education	(2) Vital Education	(3) Mental Education	(4) Psychic Education	(5) Spiritual Education

1. *Physical Stage of Education*: It includes:

(i) Total harmonious and integrated development of the body.
(ii) Physical discipline, i.e., control of various part of the body.
(iii) Freedom from diseases.

2. *Vital Stage of Education*: The vital education has two elements:

(i) Development and utilisation of senses.
(ii) Becoming conscious and gradually controlling them.

Thus vital education is very important in training senses.

3. *Psychic Stage of Education*: The word 'psychic' implies sensitiveness relating to non-material. Psychic education, therefore, implies education which includes development of non-material values. In the words of Mother, an outstanding disciple of Sri Aurobindo, "One thing is absolutely indispensable, the will to discover". Psychic is related to Yoga.

4. *Mental Stage of Education*. Mental education has the following aspects:

(a) Development of power of attention and concentration.
(b) Development of the capacity to expand mental horizon.
(c) Development of the capacity to enrich mental horizon.
(d) Development of the capacity to organise ideas around a central theme.
(e) Development of reasoning power so as to accept desirable thoughts and reject undesirable ones.

(f) Development of the power to accept or reject ideas coming from different quarters.
(g) Development of the power to get inspiration from the higher regions of the being.

5. *Spiritual Stage of Education*: This is the highest level of education. It is also called 'super-mental education'. This stage is reached after one develops physical, vital, mental and psychic elements. According to Mother, "It will, by its all powerful action, work not only upon the very substance of which they are built and upon the environment in which they live". This requires deep and intensive insight and persistent efforts. This leads to 'eternal bliss'.

MEASURES FOR ACHIEVING THE ENDS OF INTEGRAL EDUCATION

Following are the measures suggested by Sri Aurobindo:

1. Role of the Teacher: According to Aurobindo, "The teacher is not an instructor or task master; he is a helper and a guide. His business is to suggest".

2. Principles of Education: Sri Aurobindo enumerated the three principles:

(i) The teacher's work is to suggest and not to impose principles on the minds of the students.
(ii) The second principle is that the child has to be consulted in the growth.
(iii) The third principle is to work from the near to the far.

3. Discipline: Aurobindo wrote, "If education is to bring out to full advantage all that is in the individual child, we should first generate a safe custody of all that is in the individual. The divinity in man is not to be insulted".

4. Moral Training:

(i) It should be through personal example of the teacher,
(ii) '*Sadhna*' should be the basis of moral training,

(iii) It should be based on practical opportunities,
(iv) It should come through Yoga.

5. Immense Faith in the Potentialities of the Child: Teacher must have an immense faith in the capacity of the child.

6. Physical Education: Perfection or integral development is the true aim of all culture. Therefore, the physical part of it cannot be left aside. Sri Aurobindo refers to the old Sanskrit adage '*Sariram Khalu Dharma – Sadhanam*' – the body is the means of fulfilment of '*dharma*'.

7. Curriculum at the International Centre, Pondicherry: It includes:

(a) Psychic and spiritual studies
(b) Academic subjects
(c) Physical and health education
(d) Cultural activities like art, music, drama
(e) Vocational training
(f) Education for international understanding

8. Basic Principles of Integral Teaching-Learning: Integral teaching-learning process involves the following elements:

1. *Sense Training*: Sense training is developed through observation of natural phenomenon under the guidance of the teacher.
2. *Developing Power of Investigation*: Observation plays an important role in developing power of investigation.
3. *Training of Memory and Mind*: Training of memory and mind is done by equipping the students to note similarities and dissimilarities.
4. *Training in Making Judgements*: The above factors provide suitable training in making judgements.
5. *Training of Logical Faculty*: This depends upon:
   (i) Ascertaining correctness of facts.
   (ii) Collecting accurate data.
   (iii) Sifting facts by eliminating false elements.

6. ***Training of Imagination***: Training of imagination depends upon the following three elements:
   (a) Forming correct images.
   (b) Developing power of creative thinking.
   (c) Training in appreciating the existence of truth, goodness and beauty of soul in all existing things.
7. ***Training of Language***: This is done through appropriate methods of teaching and also through concrete things.
8. ***Free Environment***: Sri Aurobindo has stressed the significance of free environment under the guidance of the teacher.

CONTRIBUTION OF SRI AUROBINDO TO EDUCATION

The Ashram School: The school was originally started in 1943 for the children of Sri Aurobindo's disciples. It expanded gradually from a Primary School to a full-fledged High School. There are resident as well as day-students.

The International Centre of Education: The objectives underlying the centre are:

1. To evolve a system of education for making it dynamic, ideal for society.
2. To organise an environment which may provide inspiration and facilities for the exercise and development of the five aspects of personality—the physical, the vital, the mental, the psychic and the spiritual.
3. To emphasise the unity of all knowledge.
4. To develop the sense of oneness of mankind.
5. To discover and prepare for the role India has to play in the formation of the new international harmony.

Summing up: To understand the concept of integral education as propounded by Sri Aurobindo, we must understand the interrelationship among the different elements within the man, the nation and the universal humanity. We must see the synthesis among these.

